States of Change

Dear Carol & John

This feels like a

long time ago....

Maybe 1993 could be

as good as 1989 - Can't

be worse than 1992, can it?

Much love

[illegible]

STATES OF CHANGE

A Central European Diary · Autumn 1989

LYNNE JONES

THE MERLIN PRESS
LONDON

First published by The Merlin Press Ltd
10 Malden Road
London N.W.5
and printed by Biddles Ltd,
Guildford, Surrey

FOR TOMAZ

Author's Note

A journal is always partial and never finished.

As I edit the manuscript the crown is restored to the Polish Eagle, the two Germanies move irrevocably towards unification, the Romanian National Salvation Front is accused of lack of democracy and in Kosovo in Yugoslavia, Albanians demonstrate for human rights. The death toll increases daily but the demonstrators, mostly village people, say they have seen the Czechs on television and know they will win . . .

This journal arose out of the need to keep a log, while doing research into New Social movements in Poland. With the quickening pace of events it rapidly took on a life of its own, becoming a way for me to absorb and try to understand what was happening around me. The second part covers a journey south through Eastern Europe to a friends' home in Slovenia.

There is no attempt to give a political overview. What I hoped to do was sketch in some of the detail behind the headlines and convey the discussions, arguments and concerns of people not always in the mainstream or political limelight, but just as caught up in the process of transformation as those who were.

Without the generous financial support of the John D. and Catherine T. Macarthur Foundation, I would not have had the opportunity to be in Poland at such an extraordinary time. I wish to thank them. I also wish to thank Krystina and Jan Litynski, Sofia and Sigismund Gadaj. Without their friendship and kindness, my life in Poland would have been a lot less comfortable and my understanding of events far more limited.

Thanks are also due to Nicky Maine, Borat Cajnko, Suzanne Wasley and Matthew Sharp for help in producing a manuscript at incredible speed, to Anja Marzec-Manser and Anthony Pospieszalski for checking my Polish.

To Cvetka Sokolov and Matjas Mastnak for giving me a home, while editing. To Mark Thompson for practical and moral support, and to my publisher, Martin Eve and all at Merlin for encouragement and advice.

Most important of all and too numerous to mention, are all my friends and acquaintances in Central Europe who have allowed me to share their lives, both this autumn and in previous years. Any insights I have gained into what is happening in their half of Europe, are entirely due to them. Any mistakes in the recording of events are, of course, my own.

Finally, thanks to Tomaz Mastnak for making me write it down.

Part 1: Poland

Saturday September 30th
Gdansk

"Excellent, come and live here, there is plenty of space!" Giedymin remarked when I said that I was in Poland for three months. "Now we have democracy, everyone is leaving. Have you seen the adverts in the papers? 'Electronics engineer wants job in West, will do anything.' They'd pay to go." Giedymin is a silversmith. He lives in an old apartment in Wrzeszcz with his two children, two large Rotweilers and a recently acquired baby Rotweiler. He has no intention of leaving in spite of the fact that he has just obtained a passport for the first time in eight years. He seemed a little cynical about his fellow countrymen. "I never really liked 'the masses'. Don't believe it when they tell you about poor hungry Poles – they are greedy, complaining, and lazy and selling meat, cheese and eggs in West Berlin."

Domenica, his daughter, was doing her homework. I stuck my head round her door to say hello. She's an attractive 17 year old who who dresses in black and changes her hair colour frequently. The walls of her room are decorated with the lyrics of various punk and heavy metal groups. She introduced me to her new pet rat and seemed delighted that I had brought her "real stockings", unobtainable in Poland, rather than tights.

I have spent the day catching up with old friends. None of them are euphoric about their new government. Ania told me that it is the first time she's ever been frightened that they won't have enough money to feed the children properly. Her husband, Adam Gosiewski, has a relatively lucrative job at one of the new, private,

English language schools that are springing up everywhere. She herself is a doctor but cannot get a job because posts are frozen due to lack of funds. Adam's comment on the recent change of government is that the situation resembles a game of musical chairs, when the music has stopped, but no-one has taken any chairs away.

Maria used to be Chief Interpreter for Solidarity in 1980/81. Now she lives on her pension in a one room apartment and caretakes part-tme in the nurses hostel that occupies what was once the trade union headquarters. She went down to the new offices to offer her services. "First they told me it was too soon, then when I went back they told me: it's too late. It's not the same as when Lis was around. In those days we all worked for nothing, now they just think about money." Maria's pension is 70,000 zloties a month (£7 at black market rates). A kilo of meat is 10,000, sugar 2,000 when you can get it. "My dear," Maria exclaims in her French accented English, "we longed for this government and now it is worse!" She sat enthroned on the large bed that takes up a large portion of her living space, beautifully dyed red hair shining in the lamp light, Pony, her small dog curled up beside her. The room is a great clutter of objects covering every available surface: jars of face cream, piles of paperback novels, china ornaments. "Lech Walesa? He's got so fat! Like Jerzy Urban. And his moustache is white. When I saw him on TV with Jaruzelski I thought it was the end of the world." She asked if I knew that Walesa now had a villa in Oliwa with twelve rooms and a gardener?

Sunday October 1st
Gdansk – a.m.

Yesterday T. and I took five of us out for dinner for 30,000 zloties. Half Maria's monthly pension or £3, depending on how you look at it. I am finding it hard to adjust to my position of wealthy foreigner! This morning when we were walking with Maria in the old town, on two separate occasions, children ran up to us and said "give me something". They were quite smartly dressed and didn't look poor or hungry, they just felt 'entitled'. Maria said she felt ashamed.

Moral ambiguities aside, it is nice to be able to take friends out.

Adam Jagusiak and Margosza Tarasiewicz had just come back from West Berlin. They also have passports and are travelling as much as possible. I have known them for three years since we met at a conference organised by Wolnosc y Pokoj (WIP Freedom and Peace) in a church in Warsaw. At that time WIP, with its non-violent direct actions, its antimilitarist and ecological demands, was the most visibly active opposition group. A structureless, pluralistic network of young people, they were the first to succeed in bringing independent East Europeans from other countries together in an unofficial seminar.

WIP achieved some of its goals even before the change of government. Alternative service was introduced, the demand for allegiance to the 'fraternal armies' of the Soviet Union was dropped from the military oath. The nuclear power plant at Klempicz was halted. Now, in the new political environment, it is having difficulty finding its place. "WIP's very schizophrenic at the moment," Adam said. There were conflicts over how structured the movement should be, and between those supporting parliamentarism and those against it. "Radek Gawlik from Wroclaw WIP and Jan Rokita from Krakow are deputies to the Sejm now. They were endorsed by Solidarity of course, but they used their WIP credentials. Suzanna Dabrowska is a leading light of the Polish Socialist Party. "Democratic Revolution PPS-RD, one of its six fractions, the revolutionary Leninist one," Gosia added, "they called for a boycott of the elections."

"You wouldn't recognise her, she has a small baby, waves the red flag and sings revolutionary songs," said Adam. "Guido and Roland have emigrated to the USA." Meanwhile, some COs were picketing the parliament and on a hunger strike because the conditions for alternative service were so bad. "The law is abused. There is no information, people are cheated, sent miles from their homes and paid appallingly 12,000 zloties!" Adam said. In Gdansk, as in other places, WIP was setting up counselling offices with legal help. "The work is less glamorous and more concrete. We can't sit on a roof with banners in the morning and be reported on Radio Free Europe in the afternoon anymore." They were also organising against Zarnowiec, Poland's first and as yet unfinished nuclear power plant.

Zarnowiec is situated some miles from the triple city of Gdansk, Sopot, Gdynia. Built in an area of seismic instability and next to a culminant power plant, it almost certainly breaks international regulations. The building is of the PWR (Harrisburg model) and has been plagued by spiralling costs. Only 15% has been completed in the last 7 years, at the cost of 120 million US dollars. WIP initiated weekly demonstrations in Gdansk in February of this year and petitioned for a referendum on nuclear power. The new government has put the project 'on hold' while it decides what to do.

We walked back to their apartment: old fashioned and roomy with books and leather armchairs, it belongs to Gosia's grandmother who lives in the United States. Like many of my friends, they have a variety of jobs – translating, freelance journalism, and currently a new private enterprise of turning the front room into an art gallery. They wanted to show alternative culture from other parts of Eastern Europe. But it was taking time to get a new front door made.

Monday October 2nd
Warsaw

I have acquired a room in Warsaw or rather, three connected ones, plus a front door with four locks. It is in a pre-war apartment building in Ochota. The district is poor but neighbourly. There is a church at the back with a tree-filled yard. My street has a general store, greengrocer, bookshop and a number of specialist shops selling the sort of things you know you will need one day but not right now: dog leads, parts for televisions, sanitation equipment, felt slippers. There is also a tailor, a rarity in Warsaw these days, according to my friends. Communism provided little opportunity for the skilled artisan.

Giedymin is quite wrong. There are plenty of poor people here. I see them all the time: the old lady standing next to me in the queue at the grocers, in tailored coat and velvet hat, who found six hundred zloties too much for a piece of cottage cheese (5p at current black market rates); the old man who rummages in the bins behind the apartment building. They have pale, lined, crepey faces, the clothes are 'good' but worn. They creep around the edges of this society with none of the assertiveness of their counterparts in London or New York. These aren't bag-ladies or schizophrenics, just elderly people finding it hard to cope.

Tuesday October 3rd
Warsaw

Went round to lunch with Magda and Jacek Czaputowicz. Both were welcoming as ever but as usual it was hard to get a glimpse of Magda who was preoccupied with four children and the food.

Jacek was one of the founders of WIP though now no longer involved. "I hear you publicly confronted Lech Walesa on his accepting the presidency of the Polish Peace Council," I said. Many people had felt it was an extraordinary decision of Walesa's, given the Peace Council's Communist Party sponsorship, and consequent lack of credibility. It had not publicly supported those jailed for conscientious objection for example. "I felt I had to do it, and the National Citizens Committee was the only place available. Of course he felt exposed and did not like being attacked. Perhaps he genuinely thought WIP would welcome it. People see now that it was a stupid decision. Not the first or last that he has made."

This of course precluded Jacek running as a deputy which would have required a photo of Lech shaking his hand, but he is not sure he would have wanted to. Jacek is such a genial, friendly person it's impossible to tell what is moral stance or political shrewdness. Mostly it seems to be both.

We talked about the European Citizens' Peace Assembly, a project proposed by Charter 77 and being discussed by a number of East and West peace and human rights groups. He had been to a recent meeting in Krakow and wanted to know why Westerners kept bringing up "sexual problems". He was referring to the controversy over including the rights of sexual minorities in the founding declaration. "In the West, maybe, but don't you understand Lynne that if you insist on this it will make it completely impossible to combine with Romaszewski's Human Rights conference, he told me so. It's completely unacceptable to Poles! No one is interested!"

"I think Clause 28 made many of us realise . . ." I started to say. Jacek interrupted, "I know what you are going to say and I agree, but here it's different, it's not a priority!" He sounded quite upset.

"How often have people in WIP been told that military service, or nuclear power, were 'not priorities at the moment', yet you insisted and look what you achieved and how often have East European human rights activists criticised Western peace movements for saying human rights were 'not a priority' compared with nuclear disarmanent? I think it has more to do with primitive fears than priorities". I was getting heated myself.

"For me it's simple," T. said quietly. "In Krakow people sat in a room discussing human rights with others who could not acknowledge their real identities without fear. You cannot ignore the rights of *any* minority. If you ignore one human right you might as well ignore them all". We ate our dumplings in silence. "And in saying that a discussion of homosexuality is 'politically inappropriate'," T. added, "you are arguing in the same way as the Communists did when dismissing Human Rights as 'bourgeois concerns'."

"You are right," Jacek said finally. "In fact, thre was a programme on television recently about a gay wedding in Denmark, so perhaps things are changing."

Wednesday October 4th
Warsaw

It's not just the business world that is engaging in private enterprise; so is the academic one. I am here under the auspices of Woytek Lamentowicz's Centre for International Studies. Woytek is a professor at Warsaw University and has established the, so far, officeless Centre as a limited company.

T.'s friend, sociologist Piotr Ogrodzinski is also thinking of setting up an independent international research centre, so we went round to discuss it. Piotr, in a baggy cardigan, with unkempt beard and smoking a pipe, looked like the academic that he is. In between discussing his project he gave us a "brief guide to the current political situation in Poland". "Basically it's a triangle: there's Lech Walesa in Gdansk trying to play politician and trade union leader. Sometmes he is more one, sometimes the other. He feels he made the prime minister, which is true. Than there's the government and

Mazowiecki. They feel their job is to govern, and to muddle through, from day to day. Third: there is the Solidarity parliamentary club, the OKP – with the people from KOR: Michnik, Geremek, Onyszkiewicz, Litynski and so on – what's commonly known as "The Family" – at its centre. None of them are *in* the government except Kuron, who got the worst job as Minister of Labour. So they feel very frustrated and all three groups jostle for power. In one sense the parliamentary group, with its eyes on future government is almost an opposition. And the trade union only has about two million members, so it's quite weak."

There were new parties forming. "The peasants could be important but they are very fragmented. The current Peasants' Party in the parliament may change to its old name and divide. Rural Solidarity is organizing itself into a party. But what makes me anxious is the growth of what I call 'Catholic National Obscurantism' – KPN (the Confederation for an Independent Poland) is now in the centre. What you have on the right is a whole number of tendencies all descended from the National Democrats before the war – who were catholic, nationalist, semifascist, in an Italian way, and antisemitic. There are some signs that they will coalesce. My fear is that given a deepened crisis, people will turn in this direction – all classes, not just workers. Rural Solidarity is an important counterbalance – they are kind of social democratic Catholics. There are Christian Democrats as well – already accepted by their Western counterparts."

Thursday October 5th
Warsaw

"Piotr, oh he is leftist", was Janek Litynski's comment when I told him who we had been talking to. Jan Litynski is a founder member of KOR, former leader of Solidarity underground, and currently a deputy in the Sejm. As a member of "the family" that Piotr had described, many outsiders would regard Janek as at least "leftward" leaning.

It is almost impossible, in present day Poland, to find a fixed point of reference from which to view the political spectrum. The PZPR (Polish United Workers Party), to quote an article in Polityka, doesn't want to be a "Leninist party" because Leninism was

Stalinised, or a Marxist party, because Marxism has failed. It wants to "work for the good of the people, not just the working class," and become a Democratic Socialist party, with a new name, programme and statutes. Janek's view is that it has ceased to exist as a party. . . . "Many of its representatives were only elected with our support and are virtually independent. There are no genuine Communists. It lost its distinctive ideology in 1986/87 and all that held it together was 'Power'. Now it's lost that, it's dissolving before our eyes." While in the parliament even those with what Janek calls a "social democratic perspective" like Riszard Bugaj, chairman of the parliamentary economic commission, support the "moderate liberal tendency" that's dominant. "They all supported the new budget. There is no choice. It's a paradox but really there is no 'political opposition' at the moment. It's ridiculous – we have pragmatic problems: which technical solution is the best, but not political ones. There is no debate on whether to change the system, just how to do it."

I first met Krysza Litynski in 1982, when she was living with her spaniel in a one room flat on Mokotowska. Janek, her husband, was underground and only "appeared" in 1986. And now "we lead such a normal life," said Krysza, "Janek has a job, he goes to work, I go to work, we come home in the evening. It's very strange." Normal life means a constantly ringing phone, an endless stream of visitors and Rock music. Janek's collection of tapes and records vie for wall space with an enormous quantity of books. And just now, a very large and apparently famous, Polish rock musician who looked straight out of the Blues Brothers, was visiting, wanting contacts in the United States. He took the fact that I didn't know him with good grace. After he had left we went back to conventional politics again.

Janek felt quite happy about Solidarity's decision to go into government. "It's much simpler. Every agreement made at the Round table had to be ratified in parliament so we thought we might as well have the discusson inside as out, it's much more civilized." He personally had turned down a position as vice-minister of Labour. "I didn't want to give up my post as a deputy. And as adviser I can observe what I am doing. Maybe later – now I want to organise an office that can cooperate with the trade unions, give them an image of a modern Trade union."

He agreed with Piotr that there were difficulties between the

Trade union and parliamentary club of Solidarity. "But Solidarity was always more than a union – it was a national, social movement for freedom. The thing was the political work was organized on a trade union basis and that has now shifted to parliament." He felt that what both the parliamentary group and the Trade union should be doing together was organising as a political movement for local elections. "The real change has not occurred yet. We don't have democracy from below." Nor could they obtain it until "we change the law and have authentic self government." Moreover they wanted to challenge the conventional political model. "We would like to form political movements on the basis of local problems, around local issues, ecology and so on. We want to avoid the situation where political parties are created on the basis of traditional ideological divisions: Christian democrats, national democrats, social democrats. This might be a way of enriching parliamentary democracy – by organising on the basis of concrete problems and thus combining it with the social movements who organise around these issues."

"But how acceptable will that be to traditional parties – already waiting in the wings", I asked. "At the local level they might form coalitions. The fact is that if we fail to create political organisations of a new type, populist nationalistic movements will take over the scene. There's a far greater number of small parties connected with the traditional political right – racist, antisemitic and so on – and in a deteriorating economic situation such demagogy is attractive."

In a way I find such gloomy prognostication more worrying from Janek, who would probably describe himself as a pragmatist, than from "Leftist" Piotr.

In a recent issue of *Acapella* (an Anarchist magazine with a wide circulation among young people) there is a reprint and critical analysis of a brochure by a J. C. Majewski: a national democrat warning Poles of the "Judeo centric", Jewish/German elite from KOR who govern Poland now and whose aim is to destroy the Polish national ethos and Catholic church and give away her territories to Germany."

The paradox of democracy seems to be that it can only really exist if it is vulnerable, that is, it coexists with all the forces that would undermine and destroy it.

And as Janek pointed out this evening, in many ways Poland is still learning democracy, it doesn't come on a plate. "We have no tradition of democratic institutions. We are learning how to form them. Take the election of the Praesidium of Solidarity's parliamentary club for example, afterwards there were numerous misunderstandings simply because the club and praesidium didn't know how to cooperate together. The temptation is to function in the same way as we did in the underground or Democratic opposition of the seventies, choose leaders by natural selection. But we have to change – from a democratic movement to a Democratic institution, to structure ourselves, organize elections. It's hard, but we must do it."

Friday October 6th
Warsaw

Konstanty Radziwill is the only prince of my acquaintance. According to Norman Davies' *Short History of Poland*, his family once had more land than the Polish crown. Kostek however, with his wife Joanna, five children and one dog, live in an apartment that would fit into half of mine. He earns about £10 a month as a doctor doing three jobs: in an emergency room at night and as a G.P. during the day, plus additional work in another clinic, and he supplemented his income this year by building a golf course in Sweden. A tall, bearded, handsome man with a gentle manner, he hadn't had time to eat his sandwiches at lunch so was eating them while I ate Joanne's beautiful applecake. "More doctors are emigrating than qualifying at present. I've no idea where most of my contemporaries are." The problem with the health service was that it was corrupt, inefficient and state run. The pay and conditions were awful and the staff totally demoralised. "Anyway, nowadays people can make a future without any qualifications at all, so why study?" I remembered Giedymin telling me about a friend of his daughter's, 16 years old and earning 300,000 zloties (£30) a month selling goods her uncle brought from the West. Personally Konstanty wasn't unhappy, largely because of the improved political situation. He was chief of his Solidarity trade union at work, an adviser to the Young Parliamentarians Club and had just come back from a speaking tour of the United States. Even so, he had some reservations. "There's an increasing lack of democracy. So many decisions made in secret and Kuron appears so arrogant sometimes. Everyone is quite bewitched by aggressive capitalism. There are 'no other options', even Sweden is seen as totalitarian." "Solidarity's strength was that it was a moral opposition," he went on, "the paradox is that it's going to put morals aside for the sake of economic efficiency."

When I got home the Finance Minister, Balcerowicz, was on television, saying that with his new economic programme there would be bankruptcies and unemployment might go up to 20%. The new government spokeswoman, Ms Niezabitowska, who looks like someone out of Cosmopolitan magazine and has a curiously expressionless face, was explaining that some East Germans who crossed the border illegally were being sent back, although they would do all they could to help those here legitimately. The fact is that no sooner do they empty the West German Embassy in Warsaw and pack off the refugees on a train, it fills up again, as in Prague. It is hard for the new government to be set this practical test in the ethics of international solidarity so early on.

I had to deliver a book to a friend of a friend this afternoon. Betty Lifton has written a biography of Dr Korczak the extraordinary doctor and teacher who accompanied his children to Treblinka in 1942. Josef Balcerak had known him well and had helped her do the research. "Come at once," he said when I rang. "I will have whiskey waiting."

It was bucketing down. Driving in Warsaw leaves me unnerved at the best of times, as conventions such as stopping at a red light don't always seem to apply. In the rain, streets become lakes and you can't see the potholes.

Josef lives on his own in a tall apartment block on Walowa, by what was once the ghetto area. He was watching satellite television and after plying me with biscuits and tea (I don't like whiskey) and showing me photos of his son and granddaughters in Canada, asked if I would like to hear *his* story. It was an odd experience, walking into someone's life without preliminaries. I had the foolish feeling that he had been sitting in his small apartment looking out over Warsaw, missing his wife who died four months ago, and waiting Ancient Mariner-like for someone to whom he could tell "his story". As with all my older Polish friends, it was worth telling.

As a child he'd worked on Dr Korczak's childrens magazine (the first of its kind) then worked as a journalist until war came and he was called up. After demobilisation he had decided to join his parents in the Ghetto. He somehow found a job making German uniforms. Transports were leaving every day from Umschlagplatz and one day it was his parents' turn. He went down with them. "They still hoped it would be some kind of work camp in Germany." Someone read out a list of names of those who should return to work, including his. "I asked my parents, what should I do?"

At this point Josef burst into tears, so I don't know what they said in reply. He insisted on going on with the story.

He survived the uprising hiding in a cellar, then hid in Praga district, hoping to join the partisans. But they were taking time deciding and he was putting his hosts at risk, so he answered a German advertisement for workers to build roads in the Crimea and Ukraine. He had Aryan papers and joined a group of Polish workers. He was almost discovered during the medical to "determine race", the Russian doctor thought he was Jewish, the German one thought not. He got a job as a clerk, as he spoke Russian, Polish and German, and somehow survived until the Russians came. "Then I presented myself to them and said I wanted to join the Polish army." Which he did, as a war correspondent, advancing with them to Berlin.

After the war he founded Poland's first jazz magazine but he told me he would tell that story another time. As I stood up to go I knocked a rosary off the wall. "I converted during the war," he said. "The anti-semitism was too terrible, I wanted more possibilities for my children, a different life."

It is not that the people I know here have necessarily more pain or tragedy in their lives than those I know at home. Losing ones' parents in a car accident is as personally devastating as losing them to a concentration camp, but Polish lives are always entangled with historical tragedies of enormous dimensions, so that the awfulness is somehow amplified and resonates. When Josef Balcerak described his parents at Umschlagplatz, I immediately saw a thousand others. Suzanna's grandmother was deported to Siberia, Elzbieta's grandfather fought in the Warsaw uprising, Maria was a courier and arrested by the Gestapo. History is not a textbook affair in this country, people carry it around in their breast pockets.

Saturday October 7th
Warsaw

T. has gone to attend a conference, with other East Europeans, on "What's Left", at the European institute, in Florence. Krysza invited me to breakfast to help me organise my life. She is a psychologist, working in children's homes and is one of those people with the rare ability of making every visitor feel like a special friend. Janek should have been at the National Citizen's Committee meeting but he was too tired, and besides, he didn't think it would be very interesting today. The citizen's committees seem to be having some kind of identity crisis. In the summer after the elections, Solidarity Trade Union National Executive Committee (KKW) disbanded the district level committees and now it has just decided to withdraw the right for the citizen's committees to use the name "Solidarity". This seems a bit like jealous pique. The local committees function all over the country, producing their own magazines, campaigning on local issues, and preparing for the local elections. People see them as Solidarity. There is also some tension between local and national level as to who selects candidates. The committees want "democracy from below". Adam Michnik, writing in *Gazeta Wyborcza* yesterday, said the choice is "democratic order or chaos". Repeating Janek's point, he argued that "Solidarity has always been more than a trade union . . ." and that "a movement which has undertaken to form a government cannot satisfy itself with being just a trade union, and a trade union which is to decide everything will no longer be a trade union."

Nor does he think the committees should fragment into different political parties. But should join to create a "civic movement called Solidarity" whose tenets "include Christian moral standards and an unconcealed attachment to the values embodied by the Roman Catholic church; the national tradition of fighting for freedom, independence and tolerance: a relentless fight for social justice, for the liberation of labour, for truth in a world of political conflicts, and for common sense in economic management . . . Solidarity is neither right wing nor left wing neither Social Democratic nor Christian Democratic. It is a new kind of movement which cannot be comprehended if you use the political language of the second republic . . ." It still sounds like a political party to me, just rather a large one.

Sunday October 8th
Warsaw

Janek and Krysza invited me to go to the free market, in Wola, with them. It is a combination of car-boot sale, church hall jumble and antique market. You can buy almost anything: nasty second-hand platform boots, parts for electric hairdryers, electronic goods of all descriptions and beautiful china, silver and old furniture. Fortunately, the law severely restricts the export of pre–1945 goods or western antique dealers would have a field day. The Litynskis were looking for a table. New furniture is expensive, shoddy and largely unavailable. They also needed a sugar bowl and Krysza had to restrain Janek from buying large numbers of beautiful silver spoons. "I don't know what it is, he's always rummaging in the cutlery at home too!" said Krysza. We found the sugar bowl and I bought a black shawl from a very nice but odd, elderly woman who kept insisting her shawls weren't good enough for me.

One has the sensation of enormous numbers of goods circulating around Poland from person to person, yet nothing being actually produced. Giedymin rages about profiteering, saying that new books are bought up as soon as they appear and sold at five times the price. Piotr says the current motto is 'buy cheap, sell expensive'; certainly 'free market' and 'shortages' are a nasty combination. My experience however is that people are simply not sure how to give anything a 'real' value at present so some goods are ridiculously expensive and some ridiculously cheap. When T. and I drove off the boat at Swinoujscie, four boys rushed up wanting to clean the car windows. The windows were filthy so I agreed, when I asked how much I owed them, they had no idea and said it was up to me – a situation ripe for exploitation for those with a mind to it.

We called in on Janek's mother Regina. A tiny white haired, bird-like woman, who, having made us all tea, accosted Janek about prices. "People are very unhappy, you are not paying doctors enough and there are no drugs!" she said. Janek sat cross legged on the double bed. "We can't keep prices down if there is nothing to subsidize them with, and if we pay doctors more then butter will cost 8,000 not 4,000. The problem is productivity."

"For 10 years you've been saying what's wrong and now what are you doing about it?"

"Well, you've been pointing out all the faults in the last 10 years as well, and I'm doing the best I can!" It was a good humoured exchange. Regina proudly pulled out the Treasury Bond she had bought recently. One of the ways the government is financing its 5 million zloty deficit is by encouraging people to buy bonds. A 100,000 zloty bond can be bought for 70,000 zloties and redeemed after 6 months at full value, a good return for the investor and a "loan" to the government. The hope is that if there's an increased demand for zloties to buy bonds it will also force down the price of the dollar.

Monday October 9th
Warsaw

This morning I went to the bank and changed money. This is a major undertaking in Poland, not a 10 minute transaction. When I got in through the rather rapidly revolving brass and wooden door of the National bank, there appeared to be some kind of a strike: a large angry crowd on one side of the counter and four disinterested looking women with their arms folded in front of stationary typewriters on the other. Luckily this wasn't my queue, but even the young woman at my desk moved in slow motion. She had a plump, pretty face, yellow pinafore and carmine nails. She looked tired and bored, as I would in her position. Balcerowicz talks about "unlocking the spirit of enterprise" so that the people will start to work more productively and efficiently, but it's hard to see why they should when he has also said that prices *will* rise and wages will not.

I then went to change my dollars into zloties. There are any number of small exchange booths around the city where you can change money indoors at the free market rate or on the street, at the black market rate (usually 100 zloties more). These exchange offices are another thing that enrages Giedymin; "Sharks – a kind of Mafia, they don't pay their taxes so the State gets nothing. I don't understand why the State doesn't buy and sell money itself at the free market rate!" Not being an economist, neither do I. I did think I would try to get to grips with the economic situation. Asking my friends produces worried looks and muttered words like 'privatisation', 'convertible zloty' and 'unemployment', so I went to see a friend at *Gazeta Wyborcza*. "Ask me about France, Hungary, Northern Ireland – please not about economics!" Marek Kosakowski said, burying his head in his hands. He has graduated from editing an underground journal to being a Foreign Editor. He thrust some articles at me which I have been trying to understand.

The basic idea seems to be that money will be saved by stopping food subsidies and issuing food coupons so that only poor people are subsidised and not the rich; reducing spending on sociopolitical organisations (State funding to the Communist Party and all its organs); cutting military spending and arms conversion: Money will be generated by abolishing monopolies and encouraging privatisation; introducing VAT and personal income tax, and increased discipline in collecting corporate taxes (Giedymin will be pleased). Inflation has to be suppressed by keeping a lid on wages, so wage indexing laws are to be changed. Balcerowicz insists that if the programme is not accepted, foreign aid will not be forthcoming, and that he is sure society will show its 'maturity and understanding'. His Secretary of State, Marek Dabrowski thinks that turning people into taxpayers will encourage society to balance the budget and to take on themselves the funding of charity, education, research etc. This isn't my experience at home. On the contrary, people think *because* they pay taxes these things should be funded by the State. Meanwhile, the Bank is still printing more bank notes, hospitals still have scarcely any drugs and the Polish Red Cross has opened soup kitchens in Warsaw.

Tuesday October 10th
Warsaw

When I called on Suzanne Dabrowska this evening, she and Piotr Ikonowicz were staring gloomily at the television as Kuron finished one of his regular explanatory chats. Jacek Kuron is Minister of Labour and no longer one of Suzanna's favourite people. "We were all in love with him once", she smiled.

"What's he saying now?"

"Nothing good" said Piotr. "We have to be active, we have to produce, wages can't go up but we need every kind of activity *except* trade union activity!" I looked around the apartment, no red flags or pictures of Trotsky in evidence, just a pleasant cluttered room with children's toys on the floor, potted plants and crowded book shelves. Suzanna looked like any exhausted young mother. Piotr made us the tea.

I now have the beginning of an understanding of the complexities of the Polish Socialist Party, at least from the perspective of the Democratic Revolution section of it. The name is important, Suzanna believes that by using an old one, that people associate with prewar struggles for justice, they get away from the bad connotations of the word Socialist, and show people that there is a traditional Polish form of socialism that's positive. She explained that Socialism wasn't a "thing" that could be "good" or "bad". "All my life I've had slogans rammed down my throat, that we were fighting for Socialism, that we were building Socialism, and we built and built and nothing changed! It isn't a value in itself, it's just a *way* of making social institutions so that they include social, human feelings. It's a way of organising to make social relationships more just."

"What about equal?"

"Equal, that's utopic, it's not possible. There are conflicts between people and you need democracy to arbitrate those conflicts."

The party formed two years ago and the main split occurred in 1988, between the reformist minded, older members on the praesidium around Jan Josef Lipski, and the younger more radical members on the Central Committee. "I couldn't believe it, we were having a council meeting and four members of the praesidium arrived and after chatting about the weather, declared that the party had to 'clean' itself of Trotskyists! The language of Stalin . . . Well of course we didn't, because we didn't have any." Two months later two parties formed and after an initial period of confusion with both calling themselves PPS, Suzanna's section added "Democratic Revolution". "They believed in reforming the system, seeing Solidarity as a social movement, not a trade union. They supported Walesa, agreed with conversations with the Communists. We wanted Solidarity as a 'trade union' to fight for people, to stick with the factory committees. We didn't believe in reform.

I think it's the first time an oppositional political group in Poland has criticised Capitalism and written about third world problems in its programme." The programme also included demands for demilitarisation, and an improved environment, and protested against the selling off of national assets. "Everyone's doing it – the Communists and now Walesa. He's sold a shipyard. He didn't need to, it was a political decision."

The main focus however was on self management. The workers should, through self management committees, decide for themselves who would be manager, whether to close the business or collaborate with western capital. This was "group" ownership not State ownership. Though she admitted they did now have a Trotskyist fraction who wanted some kind of state property. "It's a minority," she sighed, "but they insist. So far, our constitution allows for fractions." The workers committees would also elect representatives to a third chamber in the government. No, this bore no relationship to the communist concept of a "workers state". "There the idea was to have only Soviets, *only* delegates from factories and the army. We want two chambers: a self management one and a political one, to represent all the interests of society, because every society has two sides."

And the Round table process? "It was boring like the Brazilian soap opera running at the time, called 'In the stone circle'. This was a circle too. After a few weeks no one had any idea what was going on, who was who, what had been decided." She was furious that the relegalisation of Solidarity had not included the right to strike, and saw the elections and the government that followed as a betrayal. "We called for a boycott of elections because we didn't want to elect Jaruzelski."

"But, Suzanna, isn't it a bit better than what you had before?" I asked. "What was the alternative to the round table?"

"If the strikes last year had gone on longer maybe by now we would have representatives from the factory committees in Parliament, and the workers themselves could decide where and when they would lose money. This is not South Korea and the IMF cannot treat us as though we were. People will not work twelve hours a day without rest; even if it was moral, it would be impossible here because this is another society here, with other standards and values."

"Of course it's very nice that some newspapers can be published openly but that's democratisation, not democracy. Take television and radio. The government said it would be under parliamentary control, in fact now it is to be under the government. All that happened is a changing of elites. Do you know how political jokes begin now? Mazowiezcki, Gorbachev and Bush instead of Gierek, Brezhnev and Carter as ten years ago. Nothing has changed! Can you see? Already in factories people start to call the government 'they'. The only chance is to show people that they can have some influence . . ."

I felt a little overwhelmed, as I always do in the face of political certainties, whatever their colour. "And something else is happening," Suzanna continued, "it's very interesting. All these other opposition groups, fighting Solidarity and so on, day by day they shift to the right – you know, completely for privatization, of course, and 'Poland for the Polish'. I see some of my friends, workers, whom I worked with in the underground, saying 'see now we have Jews ruling Poland . . .' I'm afraid we will have a movement who will say 'we want someone strong, someone responsible, someone who will make it clean here . . .' It's very dangerous . . . I am afraid."

Zusza, her daughter was crying and she got up to check.

"How do you have time for politics," I asked when she came back.

"First I have a baby, second I have a baby," she laughed. "But I fight with Piotr, all the time, from the moment she was born, so he can do everything, bath her, change her nappies. He's a very unusual man. Many people are shocked. Our latest agreement was that I should have one day a week for my work. Of course I would like three."

She was forming a women's section in the PPS party. "It's very important especially in this economic situation." The party had about 1,500 supporters and 400 activists. "Women are about a third of the party and the council so it's not too bad. They wanted to put that they were fighting for Women's Rights in the founding declaration. I wouldn't let them because they weren't and I didn't want it to be just a slogan. The Section may make it real. It's very hard being a politically active woman in Poland. Feminism still means an angry woman beating men on the head with umbrellas, you know, like suffragettes."

"Do you see yourself as a feminist?"

"Yes, in that I want to fight for women's rights, but I didn't want to do it in another organisation. I want to do it in my own, because I think they'll agree. Besides the most serious problems facing us in Poland are common ones so it's senseless to work completely separately. The trouble is a woman has to fight *with* those men with whom she is fighting *against* something else, so she has two fights. And than there's the atmosphere, you know, the jokes . . . 'you in your women's section' . . ."

"Oh yes," I said, "I know the jokes."

Thursday October 12th
Warsaw

Anna Niedzwiecka rang and told me about the boycott of military classes at the University. The classes are compulsory if the student is to graduate and include a large amount of ideological instruction. The boycott started in Krakow and has extended to Warsaw and Gdansk. There is some friction between the organising groups: NZS (the independent students' union) has less radical demands than WIP, who would like the classes abolished, not just reformed. The boycott so far has been very successful. Students hate the classes and are happy to stay away. I would find her on the picket. When I got there, three students were folding up their banners. They had forgotten it was Army Day and classes were cancelled anyway. So they sent me off to the anti-militarist demonstration being organised by anarchists in the city centre. It wasn't difficult to locate. There is a pedestrian shopping area opposite the Forum Hotel where a woman sits inside a brand new car selling lottery tickets to eager buyers. Small caravans decorated with orange and yellow light bulbs, and the words 'Supermusic', 'Cassettes' in gold lettering, blare out their latest offerings. Private food stalls sell German coffee, Swiss chocolate, cartons of fruit juice, bananas, oranges and nuts, all for zloties, at a price.

In this setting the spiky haired, black clad, young demonstrators stood out like crows at a banquet table. After a speech through a hand held megaphone we moved off down Aleje Jerozolimskie, black flags flying, drums banging and trumpets blaring. Some three hundred demonstrators occupied the full width of one of Warsaw's main streets with police cars at front and back, bringing the traffic to a seemingly unirritated standstill. "We don't want a compulsory army," "No Warsaw pact, no NATO" . . . Two young soldiers joined in briefly until removed by their colleagues. The demonstrators marched to the Parliament where a number of them pulled out their military passbooks and ceremoniously burned them in front of an uninterested, goldbraided doorman. No one else was around and the demonstrators seemed uncertain where to go next. But, after circling restlessly, they moved of to the ministries and the army prison, ignoring police directives to "Please walk on the pavement". Impossible to conceive of this a year ago, either the police protection or the indifference of passersby.

It was growing dark, and I retreated, with a young anarchist called John, to one of those cafés with furniture that looks like it's been stolen from a Wendy house: diminutive chairs with hearts cut out of the back piece, tiny tables with check table cloths. John was very "pissed off with the minority element" who had been making Indian war cries. He was an anarchist because he liked the discussions. He was at school just now but his ambition was to get his degree and live in Australia. Not that he wanted better things for himself but it would be necessary for a wife and child. "My parents love Solidarity. My father teaches at the Polytechnic. He totally supported them in the elections. I think it was OK in the early eighties; now I don't know, I'm waiting. All they say is give us time, but some things could be changed immediately. Like school for instance. The teachers are awful, the best stay in University. Our Head is a Communist, she didn't want me to learn English. Now she says 'Communists agree with the new government and like it'. I don't believe her, no one changes their way of thinking in a few months."

I went on to 48 Wspolna for the weekly meeting of the PPS-RD. It is a private flat that functions as a meeting place/office/drop-in centre for a number of radical groups and activists. Anarchists meet here on Tuesdays at 4.00 p.m.; Socialists on Thursdays at 6.00 p.m. Their respective posters decorate the walls of an otherwise bare room where, at this moment, some thirty young men and one woman were sitting on cushions, backs against the wall. Piotr I., seated on a chair, and chairing, asked new people to introduce themselves and say why they had come. Two elderly men with professor-like appearances sat uneasily on the only other chairs. The small plump one was concerned about Poland's 'false friends', and the fact that a room in the Forum Hotel cost 165 dollars a night. The tall thin one was worried about the power of the nomenklatura and had a paper he wished to read. There was a building worker, a fine arts student who liked the newspaper, a computer programmer and six conscientious objectors. Everyone was smoking furiously and working through a tight agenda dealing with the boycott at the University; how to respond to a manipulative and indifferent press; an action against food price rises: Whether to have it in the poorer parts of the city or in the centre, "where everyone is rich and no-one cares." "Kuron is going to make the poor get poorer and the rich, richer," Piotr was saying. Another concern was the new reform movement in the Communist Party – the July 8th Movement. "They're trying to become social democrats! We should picket the meeting and let people know they're incapable of change!" There was an argument over whether they should have participated in an anti-government congress. "We are the only *real* opposition party. How could we stand with those other groups?" some asked. "It was our attempt to widen the opposition. It wasn't very successful. We wanted to talk to people in different parties, *not* the leaders, but they're all too tightly connected to their own programes." "Some KPN people were thrown out of their party for demonstrating with us."

The professor began on his paper: Balcerowicz's programme was an opportunity simply for Communist bosses to buy factories and for western capitalists to use Poland as cheap labour. Mazowiecki had no interest in destroying the nomenclatura so a free market could not work.

By 8.00 p.m., with my eyes streaming and my head aching, and the professor still talking to an inattentive audience, I was feeling a strong sense of déjâ-vu. The arguments might be right but it was all too reminiscent of those endless intense discussions in my University student union: the RCG, the IMG, and SWP . . . At that stage I hoped I might learn something, at this point I felt sure I wouldn't, at least not tonight. So I escaped into clear air.

Down in the pedestrian subways there were still old ladies selling pink roses and a few money changers looking for custom. Future members of the PPS-RD? It seemed unlikely.

I called in on Janek and Krysza before going home to bed. Both were engrossed in a British spy thriller, dubbed into Polish. Currently Polish television is indulging itself in an orgy of western thrillers, mini and maxi-serials. 'War and Remembrance' is particularly popular and woe betide me if I interrupt it on a Sunday evening. At this moment however Janek wanted to know about my interview with Suzanna. "Rubbish," he snorted at her suggestion that strikes were illegal. "In a sense they are of course, but no one is prosecuted and they are going on all the time. The plan is to re-legalise them." He himself was off to Eastern Poland the next day to negotiate with workers on strike at a state farm. "Of course Communists are all for strikes in the present situation." Nor did he think much of the suggestion of having a third house in the Parliament, elected by workers' self management committees. "Wasn't self management one of Solidarity's key ideas in the early eighties?"

"It can only work for a tiny percentage of society. The best way for workers to participate is through buying shares and if they cannot afford them, we should sell them at a price they can afford. With self management there's no chance of a profit because workers aren't interested in the enterprise, only in their own salaries. They would pay themselves higher wagers at the expense of capital investment."

"Do you really think they are so shortsighted?"

"They are not longsighted enough to see that Poland needs them to accept hardship now," he said gloomily.

"Poland is perhaps a little further from home than one's own work place," I replied. The news had come on at this point. Some prisoners appeared to be on strike. They were sitting on a roof with a Solidarity banner. "Of course some of the big industries will have to have self management. With Nowa Huta (steel works near Krakow) we have no choice." I asked him about the nomenklatura. "What we are advocating is evolutionary change. The apparatus have a chance to become normal politicians; the nomenklatura, normal managers; the police, normal police. If Mazowiecki's government fails they might succeed in organising themselves. I don't believe they will, they don't have the inner strength, but leaving them in place is an enormous risk. Our policy is risky."

Friday October 13th
Warsaw

Not a good day: I woke up to find the back window of my car smashed and first aid set and spares gone. The price of a Western number plate. Krysza arrived with comfort and chrysanthemums, red hair exactly matching the colour of the flowers. At the local police station we joined a tearful old lady waiting in the corridor. She had woken to find her car totally destroyed. The police told us there had been three similar incidents that morning, which put my problem in perspective.

Some police officers wrote an open letter to the Prime Minister recently in search of a better image. They declared their loyalty and support and said that in view of increasing numbers of crimes and burglaries, and increasing shortage of staff, the police should be depoliticised and restructured in order to increase public confidence. They wanted the political departments, established after Martial law, abolished; the security police (SB) clearly separated from the rest of the service; the Zomo reorganised; and the right to form an independent trade union. And "in order to show that the law is the same for all Poles regardless of their party membership or faith. We want not to be a Party but a State police and are returning our respective Party-cards." This caused some controversy. When interviewed they replied, "If not now when? If not us who?" And "we wanted the rank and file to help the top."

My policeman was definitely the Dixon of Dock Green type. After he had taken our coats, found us chairs, cleaned the ashtray and lit Krysza's cigarette, he took a statement. It took an hour and a half, as it required handwriting in duplicate on separate forms – the same information arranged in different ways so he couldn't use a carbon; then typing laboriously with one finger on an elderly GDR typewriter – the kind that require heavy pressure on the keys. I entertained myself staring at the poster of Bialystok Forest and two large girlie pictures – one naked brunette kneeling in the surf and one blonde in a pink mini looking out from a wood with parted lips. "Do you think you will find the perpetrator?" I asked my policeman. He roared with laughter and pointed to a stack of files.

In fact Kiszcak (Minister of the Interior) has ordered the dissolution of all Zomo riot police. In some places they are going to be made into special preventative patrols.

Saturday October 14th
Warsaw

I am becoming fascinated by the problem of political invisibility. When I explain to people that I am doing research into social movements their response is "Oh, do they exist?" Three years ago leaders of Solidarity like Janusz Onyszkiewicz and Jan Litynski pointed to groups like WIP as playing a crucial role. "They fought with this tendency to conspiracy, proved it was possible to be active in an open way which is much more efficient." Now that the mainstream opposition is in power, and concerned reasonably enough with trying to drag the country out of the economic quagmire such groups and their concerns appear marginal, if perceived at all. Geremek talked this week of "social fatigue". A journalist friend of mine present at the Round table, complained about the difference between now and 1980. "Then it was a revolution. Now it's collapse of the old system. The pressure from below is not there." Woytek Lamentowicz, a professor at Warsaw University felt that the Parliament didn't include young people in its process in any way and didn't answer their needs, which was why they were becoming apathetic. (NZS membership runs at 5–10% in most universities.)

Yet under the surface a number of small currents appear to be bubbling away, pulling in different directions. This afternoon I went to Wspolna, Krakow and Warsaw. WIP activists were meeting in one room planning to occupy the PANAM office on Wednesday (PANAM is apparently building a hotel in one of Krakow's last green spaces.) The Anarchist Intercity Federation were meeting next door. It was quite possible to tell they were Anarchists from the lack of a chair and jumbled arrangement of bodies. A man and woman were flat out asleep on a couch and everyone else was huddled up at one end of the room talking at once. They were organising a financial council and energetically rejecting the democratic centralist suggestion, that contributions from the federated groups should not be redistributed for use locally but kept to finance a journal or such like.

These are hard times for Anarchists. The state has never been more popular. Krzysztof Galinski, a tall, dark haired student who had been in and out of prison in the last few years for antimilitarist actions, pointed out that whereas last year any demonstration was good because it was "against the Communists" now "passers by stop us and complain that we shouldn't demonstrate against Solidarity and the new government." He himself found it difficult sometimes to protest against people like Michnik or Kuron who had been in prison as he had. On the other hand he found it hard to believe such people really were the same. They had become so unapproachable in government.

"Has anything improved," I asked.

He grinned. "It's like being suddenly transferred from a prison with very bad conditions to the one with very good ones. It's worse." At least before when they were arrested and imprisoned they got publicity. "Now the police no longer harass us, our problems have become non existent. They don't intervene because we have stopped being dangerous. We are becoming more and more like people in the West," he continued, "you can publish officially but no one cares, unless the problem directly threatens them. They used to disapprove of Jaruzelski. Now they accept him and authority in general. People don't need a vent for dissatisfaction anymore. It was very clever of the Communists to share power with Solidarity. Now when people complain they simply say: you can address this to the government, we are no longer responsible."

It's easy enough as an outsider to see why the new government might not regard Krzysztof and his concerns as important in the scale of things. WIP has some six or seven functioning groups and numbers a few hundred activists, Anarchist Intercity sixteen groups and similar numbers. But they appear to articulate clearly what a number of young people are feeling. Krzysztof talked of a recent television programme where young people were polled on the activities that most interest them. "Working for Peace and Freedom," was the reply. "They were not interested in any organisations but the ideals as such." When I asked Krzysztof why he was an anarchist, he replied simply "I'm involved with the problem of my own freedom and combine it with wanting freedom for others." The danger as he saw it was that while such ideas had a certain popularity in his generation at the moment, if young people continued to feel alienated they might turn to ideologies with more striking power. "Of course in one way it's natural, Poles always felt inferior, going abroad, and now they want to compensate for everything lost in the last 45 years. A special committee of the Episcopate made a statement recently saying things like "We should not adopt liberal patterns from the West, but have our own National system." Also that "every Pole was to be a catholic unless he was a Jew!"

"Nationalism is such a nice, consistent, well arranged ideology and it provides a feeling of national pride. It can draw on a centuries old tradition, not like anarchists and Pacifists who have to look outside the country for their roots." He was worried by its intellectual potential and the dangers of combining their strength and energy of young people.

Sunday October 15th
Warsaw

Krysza and I caught the bus out to a friends house in Laski today, to go mushroom picking. The woods lap round the edges of the garden and there were families of mushroom hunters everywhere, plastic bags already bulging. Margosza, however, knows the forest and we followed her into its depths, birch and oak on fire around us and the ground tawny gold. Krysza can sense eatable fungi at 100 yards; I seem only capable of finding poisonous ones. Nor did I have the deft finger movements required for making the pierogis for dinner. I was told to use a fork, as children do, to press the edges together, but retreated in shame to talk to Andrej in the living room. He is an economist. He wasn't that optimistic. Misters Sachs and Lipton, the Harvard economists, weren't right in pushing for a rapidly convertible zloty immediately. Poland should first get more domestic stability. That wasn't going to be easy. Foreigners, as individuals or governments were not rushing in with aid or investment. He wasn't surprised; no one could guarantee political stability yet, so who would want to make a long term investment. They would just be looking for quick profit. Meanwhile prices were still rising and that was clearly because people had and were using more savings than had been expected – so market forces couldn't come into play.

When we got home Janek was back exhausted from arbitrarian

efforts in Eastern Poland and trying to write a speech for a meeting of the European Assembly of the Council of Europe the following day in Sicily. The strike had ended not with the hoped for resignation of the director of the farm, but at least with a wage rise.

Monday October 16th
Bydgoszcz

Bydgoszcz is not a beautiful city. Its main street consists of shabby prewar buildings of no particular architectural merit. Most people are housed in ranks of ugly, impoverished apartment blocs, each surrounded by a no-man's-land of grey-green grass and no trees. Marek's, in particular, lies under the flight path of the airport so that regularly, every hour, one is deafened by the roar of planes. He and friends were campaigning against an extension of the flight path desired by the military. When I first met Marek three years ago, he had an organic farm. On the next occasion he was in the second month of a hunger strike and on trial for refusing military service. He was convicted and imprisoned for three years. He was released under amnesty seven months after maintaining the hunger strike but being force fed throughout. Now the farm is leased and he is trying to make money in a small "enterprise" like everyone else. "It's necessary to live," he said, it didn't leave him much time for politics but he spent two afternoons a week counselling prospective COs.

His office consisted of a table and two chairs in a small room in a barnlike, red brick church. The walls of the room were decorated with a "Stop Zarnowiec" poster and the usual Trinity of Father Popieluszko, Lech Walesa and Pope John Paul II. The room's main function was as the office for Parish Assistance and behind a large table in the centre, three women and a man dealt with an endless stream of requests: mothers with infants and babies came in for medicines; a woman asked about housing; a man just released from prison with no clothes or money needed help. Ignoring the hubbub, Marek sat with a client, a heavy featured, anxious young man, called Stefan. He had got the address from Solidarity he said. He'd failed university entrance exams and worked on the railway. He had made up his mind a long time ago that the army was "no good," having seen what happened to his friends doing military service. "A year ago they were smiling and energetic, not now." Marek explained the complex procedure, the likelihood that Stefan would be told it wasn't possible. Stefan said he was determined and wanted to join WIP as well.

It's curious that the armed forces, which have committed themselves to a purely defensive role and intend to cut troop numbers by 40,000 by the end of 1990, should still make things so unpleasant and difficult for young people who want to do alternative service, (apart from the poor pay and conditions it also takes a year longer) especially given the shortage of staff in public services like health care. Why not pay and train them as nursing auxiliaries, a lot more useful than unhappy soldiers.

Tuesday October 17th
Gdansk

One of the reasons I'm more comfortable in Gdansk than Bydgoszcz is that most of my friends have apartments in houses rather than high-rises so that life takes place in a more human scale. The buildings in Wrzeszcz and Sopot are mostly turn of the century or interwar. The facades are crumbling and poorly repainted but still elegant. Wrought iron balconies, decorated plasterwork with a fondness for vines and flowers. Anja and Adam G, with whom I am staying, live in an attic flat with porthole windows overlooking the East German Consulate. They have spent three years enlarging it to accommodate their two small boys. Eva, the previous tenant, and daughter of their landlady will be visiting from West Berlin. She emigrated in 1983 and they joke anxiously that she might like the flat so much she will want to return.

"Could you ever leave?" I asked Anya.

"I suppose if things got very bad, perhaps, for a couple of years. But this is my country, my family, my language, culture, my friends. I'm not the sort of woman who could be happy anywhere else," she replied. "I'm like most of people. I trust in the government. I'm quiet and not angry. It's difficult to do something very quickly so we have to be patient." She was pleased at the moment because there was the possibility of a job in Paediatrics at the Hospital. Though she still had to find a baby-sitter. Adam's only complaint was that the milk they had delivered to their doors was now costing

13,000 zloties for a full cream pint rather than 4,000 as it had been a few weeks ago. "I don't worry so much about my family," Anya said picking up her youngest, cherubic looking youngster to feed him, "We can go and work abroad for two months if we have to. It's old people and families with no savings."

I certainly worry about Maria. When I went round to see her I discovered she had sold a favourite jumper to a friend, who so far hasn't been able to pay for it, and she didn't know how she would manage until the end of the month. I gave her 20,000 zloties which was all I had in my purse. She gets her main meal each day at a local canteen, where she prepays at the beginning of each month so at least she won't starve. She has plenty of friends but is far too proud to ask and anyway they have difficulties too.

Gosza and Adam J. had maps all over the floor, planning their route to Holland. They were going to a conference on Conscientious objection. The problem was that Gosza hates flying. They needed an FRG visa to go by train but the embassy wasn't functioning as it is still full of East Germans. Apparently they have decided to fly them out now because people kept trying to join the train as it went through East Germany.

Gosza has been asked to be an adviser to Solidarity Trade union on "Women". "I think they felt that a 'perfect' trade union should have a women's section," she said. The initiative had first come from the International Confederation of Free Trade Unions who wanted to help women organize in Poland. "The realisation that there *is* a problem is a step forward." Her idea was to create small working groups in each region who would focus on whatever issues interested them: working conditions in the textile industry, ecology in Silesia. They could then demand political representation in each region's authority hoping both to make their problems visible and influence the politics of the union as a whole. They had been promised financial assistance, the problem was, would women themselves be interested. "Most women simply don't see themselves as exploited even when they're working night shifts at the meat processing plant here, carrying thirty kilograms loads, way above the norm."

Not everyone in the region was happy about the project. When Gosza and some friends who were in the local teacher's union, had gone to ask for a room where they could meet and have coffee, Bogdan Borusewicz, chief of Gdansk Region Trade Union had exploded, "I suppose you would like to see men giving birth to children next!" He saw no point whatsoever in a separate women's organisaton, and although Gosza had carefully avoided the word feminism in order not to discourage him, had shouted that no "Western feminist fashion would be followed in Gdansk!" Gosza had retreated upstairs to the National offices where they had told her not to worry. She could organise at National level first and perhaps Boruszewicz would come round.

Adam wanted to go down to the university. The boycott of military studies has spread to include Gdansk and he wanted to try interviewing some of the military teaching staff for *Gazeła Wyborcza*. To our surprise they were delighted to talk to us. If someone had told me, even a year ago, that I would be sitting at long table under a crownless eagle and picture of desert warfare, while two Army officers informed me that they taught their students about four kinds of pacifism, I wouldn't have believed them. Apparently, they told us, there are the Christian Gandhians who don't mind serving in the army if necessary; the "aggrieved" who are against the authorities but will defend themselves, Humanists and "Integral" pacifists who are END pacifists, and "total refusers." "What is END," I asked, astonished to hear it being taught about in Gdansk university's military studies curriculum.

"Oh, a Western antinuclear group that is now very political. We don't evaluate it, we just inform them as best we can. We have a lecture – 'Bringing up People for Peace' – but the problem is in Poland people just don't discuss this subject," said the senior, more dapper looking, blond haired officer.

He had no objection to conscientious objecting but argued that no society had completely rejected the idea of training its intelligentsia to be military minded. It was necessary for the defence of society. As Marshal Sternakowski said to the Polish senate, "It's very negative for young people to have a negative view of the army." There was no question of political indoctrination. They taught: "Methods of defence in Poland's history and the present, the structure of present forces and the obligation to defence of the Nation." "I've often thought the teaching of military history to young ladies was unnecessary, but it is needed for people going to be officers. I ask them after each training if they feel indoctrinated. They laugh at the idea."

As to the boycott. "It's not a spontaneous boycott, it's organised by NZS who support Solidarity, but we don't try to convince them one way or the other." Indeed they themselves had pinned up the demands on the noticeboard, unfortunately they couldn't show us as someone had taken them down again. It's not up to us, but the ministries of defence and education. They are discussing the matter. In my 30 years experience as an army officer the army has always been in the hands of the nation, which decides what it should do. The army is here to be ordered about, you know."

"How do you respond when students ask you about the role of the army in martial law," I asked.

"The 1792 constitution said that each nation must defend itself," the senior officer began.

"We're talking about the use of the army aganst its *own* nation," Adam interrupted.

"Martial law was a political decision, every army must do what the government says."

"Some Polish officers recently criticised the invasion of Czechoslovakia as a mistake," I said. "Do you think that officers might begin to see martial law as a mistake?" There was a long pause, then the senior one, looking grave, spoke again. "I think it's very bad when an officer tries to come to political conclusions. He should stop being a soldier. There's no place on earth where a soldier can make political decisions, he has to follow orders. Anyway," he added more cheerfully, "I'm an optimist, and don't believe there's any place in Europe where armies will have to make this sort of decision again."

"But hasn't unquestioning obedience led to some really appalling crimes? My Lei, the Holocaust . . .?" I asked.

"There are specific laws for these situations. In your country some personal dramatic decisions have to be made – Ulster, for example. I don't think British soldiers like having to pacify a strike. It's very similar, our soldiers have to follow orders. The army is a centralised institution and one has to be loyal."

"Loyal to who? Country or government?"

"Country of course."

"So could there be a situation where loyalty to country might require a decision to act against the government?"

"Oh I don't think that could happen in this country," he smiled.

It was time for us to go but the junior officer, dark haired and rather plump was very anxious that we should understand what very good relations they had with their students. "We know these rumours of negative selection, jokes that we're not capable of other work, that we would do anything to keep our cushy jobs and obstruct the boycott. It's not the case!" He looked very upset, "Every teacher is evaluated for their intellect! Besides, I've been a student myself at this university for 9 years, I understand students, I think like them." At the end of every year they received flowers and a book dedicated to them from all the students – this year Miss Polonia herself had signed. "We've seen the students have to make very dramatic choices, young ladies crying because of having to choose between loyalty to Solidarity and their private interest." He shook his head regretfully. We were being escorted out past the picture of soldiers crouched behind camouflaged artillery, popping out of tanks, firing missiles and an incongruously placed poster advertising a "Solidarity song book: Songs for Street and Home," Both officers bowed, heels together, kissing my and Gosza's hands. Out in the courtyard Adam shook himself, "Flowers, Miss Polonia! Don't they realise students want to pass their exams?" I felt a little sad.

Wednesday October 18th
Warsaw

I am sitting in a large comfortable armchair in the lobby of the hotel Victoria with my eyes glued to the entrance to the PAN-AM office, along the corridor. No sign of Krakow WIP and it is very unclear to me how they will occupy an office full to overflowing wth Polish people eager to travel to the USA.

Never mind, I am being entertained by the loud conversation taking place between the people sitting around me. There is Charlie in charcoal grey suit, fiftyish, slightly overweight American; a Czech lady, elderly but very well preserved, slim and elegant in silk blouse, heavy silver rings, leather coat, with well cut hair and carefully applied lipstick; and Pavel, tall, blond, Polish and dressed in cream suit, blue shirt, and white trench coat. Pavel was discussing the schedule for the day – an appointment at the TV studio, various meetings with "grantees." Charlie was very frustrated that at $150 a night for his hotel, he still had to walk across the square to get a *Herald Tribune* and couldn't get through to the American

Embassy on the telephone, where he was dining with the ambassador tomorrow. I have to confess some sympathy with Charlie. The Warsaw telephone exchange was last renewed, I believe, in 1955, and is having difficulty coping with new times. It's often easier to phone England than across the river.

"Communication, Pavel, Communicaton it's the heartbeat! the breath of life!" Charlie is saying. Pavel smiles apologetically. The Czech lady is emphasising the need for simple Video guides for American tourists.

"I've made countless films," says Pavel, "but Orbis (Polorbis – the Polish travel agency) didn't use them."

"On what?" asks the Czech lady sharply.

"Oh, castles, posters, churches," Pavel replies vaguely.

"But this is not what we want! A whole film on castles," the idea seems to shock her. "Americans want something simple – Krakow, Warsaw, what to see, where to go." Pavel looks disconsolate. The discussion moves onto "Art." Pavel is lamenting the difficulties of the current situation. During Martial law and after there was more money around because the West saw all art as "opposition" and funded it from abroad and because Jaruzelski saw artists as potential troublemakers and funded them to keep them quiet. Now Mazowiecki has other priorities, like food, and the West thinks there are no problems. Pavel had tentatively told the art historians, whom they would be meeting today, that Charlie might . . .

"Pavel, Pavel" the Czech lady interrupts in horror, "this is a mistake, Charlie cannot give money!"

"I have no money," Charlie says sadly, which is clearly not true, if the suit is anything to go by, but Pavel understands. "Contacts," Charlie says, "I have contacts and you will have them all." While the Czech lady apparently knows everyone on the National Endowment for Democracy, "so there is no problem at all." Pavel looks more cheerful and they move off in a flurry of expensive clothing.

By afternoon there was still no sign of action at the PAN-AM office so I went shopping. Warsaw has acquired a certain superficial gaudiness in the last year. Around Novy Swiat there is a rash of boutiques, Komis (secondhand clothes) shops and little galleries. Items jostle for space in vivid window displays. Mohair jumpers 100,000 zloties, nylon underwear 30,000 zloties, leather, jewellery, belts, bags; an undistinguished oil painting for 200,000 zloties. T.

remarked when he was here how strange it was that the first appearances of the free market were always boutiques selling useless things, never improved services or better quality food. "It is as if only the appearance and ideology of the West were for sale." Of course, if you can't find what you want and you have dollars you can always retreat to the Pewex shops which now seem to sell everything and if you have anything left after that, you can gamble it away in the Casinos which have opened in every hotel. I have the increasing sensation of living in a double world.

I got back to the Victoria to find that Krakow WIP had plastered the windows of the PAN-AM offices with posters saying "PAN-AM out of Krakow" etc. and were sitting, pleased as punch, in a row on the pavement, outside while bewildered tourists muttered "Why PAN-AM?" An emphatic young man called Staszek Zubek explained that the Krakow city council, who were "totally corrupt" were allowing the PAN-AM Hotel to be built on "the Blonia" (public grassy spaces around the old town that act as lungs in this beautiful but polluted city). A petition signed by 10,000, and the fact that Krakow is hedged with protective legislation, had had no effect, hence the action. They had decided against occupation as they were only a small group but they would be picketing the court house the next day. Staszek's father happened to own a small piece of the land in question and was contesting its compulsory purchase. Would I come and support them? I promised to try.

When I got home a woman rang asking if I wanted to come to a meeting of the Warsaw families. "Women" seem to be another of those currents rumbling under the surface. In fact women have constitutional equality in Poland. But harsh economic conditions, a traditional approach to family life and a powerful Catholic church combine to create a quite different reality. Most women do not choose whether to work or not, it is essential to generate enough income to support the family. Meanwhile shopping, cleaning and child care are still very much their responsibility. So "emancipation" is equated with a doubly heavy work load and "feminism" with a kind of foreign craziness, totally irrelevant to their situation. All the political structures: Communist Party, former opposition and now the new government are predominantly male.

But recently things have begun to change. This spring the church proposed that abortions, performed for any reason, should become a criminal offence with both woman and doctor punishable with three years imprisonment. Sex education is nonexistent in schools (a reasonable textbook was recently withdrawn under pressure from the church). Contraceptives are a scare resource unless you have the hard currency to buy "anti-baby" condoms at Pewex shops. Abortion is therefore seen as a necessary evil by many women and it is the churches initiative that appears to have kicked the beginnings of a women's movement into life. Two thousand people demonstrated in Warsaw in the spring, various women's self defence leagues were established around the country and although the proposal was shelved, the groups have continued to function.

The Warsaw Feminists have been in existence as a discussion and support group since 1980 but the abortion issue and the new political climate had made them decide to be more active. When I got there four women in their thirties were sitting around a table in a pleasant kitchen; nice women, looking and sounding very much like Western feminists, concerned whether to meet in the afternoon so that women with babies could come, or the evening so that working women could. They were also planning a demonstration for the 12th of November. Apparently an American woman had rung and asked them to support the "pro choice" demonstration on the same date in Washington. The women saw this as a good opportunity to raise the abortion issue again, as they felt the church's proposal might well be revived by catholic deputies in the new parliament. They were a little anxious as they planned to picket the U.S. embassy and no one had demonstrated outside these sacrosanct premises before.

They also planned to register as a legal association. This meant finding a treasurer. "Not that we want a formal hierarchy or anything," Ivanna explained, "but we need a place where people can meet and we can keep materials accessible to everyone."

The group had other concerns: violence against women. "There's no data, but we know it's an enormous problem just from considering the high rate of alcoholism in this country," Jola said. And pornography: "It suddenly seems fashionable to have lots of pictures of almost nude women all over the newspapers," she added. Officially pornography is forbidden. They were mostly professional women, psychologist, translator, university teachers. Jola echoed Gosza's view that working women didn't see themselves as particularly exploited. "They have often organised together but paradoxically it sometimes appears to be in support of their own exploitation." She told me about women working night shifts at Warsaw steel works. This is illegal under international regulations. The management decided to move them to day work. The women organised a protest, pointing out that while they were paid less than men doing night work they were paid more than women on day shifts. The hours gave them a chance to be with their children and besides "they had worked the shifts for so long that they didn't need much sleep."

Thursday October 19th
Warsaw

Sosia, my interpreter has Sky television. She teaches English at the Economics institute and feels the opportunity to have spoken English in her living room justifies the expense of the satellite dish. This means I can watch English news, courtesy of Rupert Murdoch. Some kind of slow fuse seems to be burning in Eastern Europe. Honecker has resigned after weeks of demonstrations in the GDA, and Hungary is no longer a "people's republic," a step Poland has yet to take.

Sosia is a delight, small, dark haired. She worries constantly that I am not eating enough, and is endlessly helping me sort out the hassles of day to day life. The only favour I am allowed to do in return is perfect her already excellent English grammar. After checking some exercises she had written for her students and being plied with apples and tea I walked the two blocks home, navigating round the heaps of coal that suddenly fill the street.

Saturday October 21st
Warsaw

There's a joke a Polish friend told me, that if you put two Poles on a desert island there will be three newspapers and none of them will agree. I spent four hours at a gathering of the representatives of various environmental groups today feeling that, much as I hate national stereotypes, this joke had some aptness.

The meeting took place in the back room of the Dominican church in the Old town. The discussion was initially on how to prepare for the local elections and "keep environmental issues on the agenda." This got very muddled with another discussion as to how to set up some form of environmental "police force." Should they trust the National Commission on the Environment to choose people: no, there should be a "citizens' movement from below, one couldn't trust the government;" yes, because "we now have a government that's good and shouldn't fear government control." Should the volunteers be the old, already existing "inspectorate?" Who would train them? Should they be the candidates for the local elections? We shouldn't have candidates, just support those who adopt our platform – we don't have a platform yet – we need "a list" of candidates.

The participants, around sixty of them, were of all kinds and came from all over the country: WIP activists like Staszek, very pleased because his father had won his courtcase, an unprecedented victory. Members of the various fractions of the Green Party, mostly in ties wearing traffic light badges. University professors, members of KIK, the catholic intelligentsia club, one parliamentary deputy: Radek Gawlik.

Radek is an interesting man in his early thirties, he straddles the uneasy divide between movements and parliament. He had been active on environmental issues in Wroclaw WIP from its foundation and saw standing as a deputy as a practical way of taking these issues further. Wroclaw, as Radek told me is one of the pollution hot spots in Eastern Europe. The air is poisonous, and the river contaminated with carcinogens and raw sewage. It also has a higher rate of birth defects than other cities, something Radek finds particularly worrying with a new baby on the way. "This country is dying," he said. "That's our basic problem." Recently the young conscientious objectors picketing the parliament had asked him to negotiate for them. I am told they chose Radek rather than Jan Rokita, another former WIP activist, because Jan Rokita wore a suit and Radek didn't. He hadn't been very comfortable with the job, feeling that they were asking for too much, too quickly and, when something was achieved, escalating their demands.

Now he was mildly suggesting that the ecological groups needed some common points for the election but that a national list of candidates was foolish as each region had specific local problems. "We also desperately need a secretariat first, to ease the flow of information." The discussion went around in circles a few more times. "Don't forget the disabled!" "We could use health inspectors for nature." I and a friend decided to retreat to a cafe. As we were leaving, a man from one of the fractions of the Green Party was saying – "we need *one* ecological lobby in this country to have more power." Radek appeared to have buried his head in his arms. "The Green Party," my friend Tomas Terlecki said in scorn over lunch, "is like a headmaster looking for pupils. Movements need to be created from below, don't they? Well some people wanted to be very important, so they built a party from the top down. Quite a lot of us did join at the beginning. At the first congress there were three spokespeople with equal power, now there are three fractions. Most of us left. There are about seventy people in it now, I think." Many of them joined the Green federation, a network of autonomous local groups whose organising principle appeared to be that the roots of ecological disaster lay in hierarchical society being organised in monolithic structures. There was no point, therefore, in repeating the pattern. Tomas had no idea, consequently, how many were involved but Krakow was very active. There were at least a hundred different ecological groups in Poland, he told me.

"The thing about this government now is that it might respond to pressure; so we should press, but everyone's waiting."

"Are you waiting?" I asked.

"No, I'm organising a foundation to support all these movements. One thing we all need is money."

Sunday October 22nd
Warsaw

I had a sudden longing for an English newspaper and went out to the Marriott hotel to find one. I drive past this monument to joint ventures everytime I go into the centre. It strikes me as singularly appropriately placed, just across from another monument to another time: the Palace of Culture, Stalin's "gift" to Poland in the fifties when they were rebuilding their country out of the rubble. Of course the Palace is a pale neostalinist grey, while the Marriott is shining glass that reflects the sky – unfortunately today also dirty grey. Never mind, inside all was warmth, light, greenery, live orchestral music from the Viennese cafe and an overwhelming number of mirrors. It is hard to pin down the design concept – art nouveau, postmodern, neoclassical, but it is definitely luxurious.

I couldn't find a newspaper so ended up buying the *Warsaw Voice*, an English language weekly that's been running for over a year now. Appropriately enough they had a report on the LOT-Ilbau-Marriott enterprise. LOT have half the shares; Ilbau, an Australian building firm and Marriott 25% each. The building houses an air terminal and offices. I now know that it has 650, 12 channel, TVs; 23 lifts, two telephone exchanges servicing 3000 phones (a friend told me it has its *own* satellite connection to the U.S. so you can call there direct, but Warsaw is still a problem) and that King Juan Carlos of Spain had *everyone* who was anyone (Mazowiecki, the cabinet, Jaruzelski, the PZPR (Polish United Workers' Party), Drawicz and Urban (present and former heads of radio and television) to a banquet where he served smoked donkey as a Spanish speciality.

More to the point. Cloakroom attendants earn 232,000 zloties a month before tips and get two meals a day. That is the lowest wage. The highest is 1,026,000 zloties. Employees apparently carry out their work "efficiently, with precsion and in a mood of joy." They have all been taught to smile. Who would want to be a doctor?

Inside the paper they had an article on poverty; I gathered more statistics. Free meals are now distributed at nine locations in Warsaw, more are needed, but apparently people have not yet re-acquired the prewar habits of charity. It is the elderly themselves who contribute most. Retail food prices rose three or four times in August and the Central Planning Office states that if the prices continue to spiral at the same rate annual inflation could reach 5,600%. The Institute of Social affairs says the minimum each person needs simply to buy food is 75,000 zloties, whereas the average pension was 68,486 zloties in August. Kuron has promised supplementary index linking of wages to protect the poorest; to maintain pensions at last year's level; and to provide food coupons. But the authorised printing works has said it can't handle the coupons as it is too busy printing money.

Monday October 23rd
Warsaw

My computer printer decided not to work today and in despair I rang up a friend at *Gazeta Wyborcza*. "Come and use ours!" he said immediately. Hard to imagine a similar response from the *Guardian* – "yes, but at home you would simply get the printer fixed," Krysza said. I'm not sure if a friendly network of mutual aid doesn't actually have some advantages over "better services." The question is will the former disappear with the introduction of the latter?

The *Gazeta Wyborcza* offices run in a railway track arrangement of low ceilinged, thinly partitioned rooms at the base of a large apartment building on Iwicka. At least half the staff appear to be in their twenties and there is an air of friendly informal chaos more reminiscent of a student magazine than a professional newspaper. No shortage of computers though. My friend Jacek Fronczak started there cleaning windows, before graduating to journalism. In fact he is a historian and had written a book on the Soviet Occupation of Poland in the second World War. "Previously I was a bit of a hero, now it's quite normal to do it," he joked.

Until a month ago the paper had a history page. Then Helena returned from the United States, saying that the most important thing in a daily newspaper was daily news so the page was cut and he had moved to features. I had met him originally because he was wandering around carrying plastic carrier bags advertising an AIDs helpline – not a common sight in Poland. He was completely incensed by a scaremongering, ill informed article he had read in another paper and was writing a feature in reply. Professor Stapinski, the AIDs expert in Poland had given him the bags. Anyway the features department appeared to be contracting as well, so today he wasn't so happy. "The problem is paper and ink, we are still fighting with *Zycie Warszawy* for readers and we only have eight pages." He also felt the paper was increasingly less independent.

"Before we had the new government, it was excellent, *really* independent. It filled a gap in society and was an enormous success. Since the Mazowiecki government we've started to make politics. Our very first meeting after the election we were told: OK, we are going to be critical but not yet, the government needs time. It's hard when you are writing something to be told it's not time for it yet." He gave an example of the coverage of September 17th, the anniversary of the Soviet invasion. "Everyone has always commemorated it with flowers. So we made the observation that no one from the church hierarchy or new government had done anything to mark the day. The article was stopped. The main problem is having a politician as main manager. Adam Michnik shouldn't occupy such a prominent position – it means the paper, whether he likes it or not, is seen as his mouthpiece and our hands are tied accordingly. If he is about to visit the Ukraine we can't be too critical of the Soviet Union and so on."

Paradoxically, *Gazeta Wyborcza* recently challenged Lech Walesa in an interview, on limiting the independence of the press. He had, without consultation with the editorial team, appointed his "own" man, Jaroslaw Kaczynski to be editor of ," *Tygodnik Solidarnosc.* Walesa unashamedly argued that "this is a time when loyalty is needed. It is too early (for an independent press)." His concern was to create "political equilibrium" with a more trade union oriented publication to balance the other political forces in society. That is the new government and parliamentary group of Solidarity. "There must be equilibrium between left and right, when one becomes too strong I will support the other."

We were wandering from office to office in search of a compatible programme. Jacek said he and friends dreamed of starting a "really" independent paper. Currently it was just a dream. "A few years ago I wanted to leave. I am more optimistic now, not that it's any easier to obtain the necessities of life, but there's hope."

I got home to find a friend sitting on the staircase. Neil had been in Prague at a meeting to discuss the European Peace Assembly. It had been the usual scenario of meeting places switched at the last minute, some Czechs unable to participate because of being followed in the street, though for once Sabata had managed to attend. Neil had asked Martin Palous, a former Charter spokesperson, how long he thought things could go on in this way. "Less than a year," he had replied.

Saturday October 28th
Krakow

Krakow is a city that always seems to require superlatives. It is arguably the most beautiful city in Poland and also has some of the most unbreathable air. My throat is dry and irritated after just a few hours. During Martial law it had some of the ugliest confrontations between the police and nonviolent demonstrators at Nowa Huta, the steel works, outside the old city. More recently there was a large demonstration outside the Soviet consulate demanding "Soviet troops out."

The KPN (Confederation for an Independent Poland) has some of its most active support here. Leszek Moczulski, its leader, stood in the election, against the Solidarity candidate, Jan Maria Rokita. Rumour has it that Rokita was so concerned about his chances that he made "inappropriate" use of donated funds to wine and dine his potential supporters. But then Krakow is rife with rumours. Too many "political personalities" for one small town.

What's also clearly demonstrated here is the way increased political space has resulted in a process of fragmentation. There is now room for each "personality" to have his own political group. What's more, following a tactic adopted countrywide by the KPN in the last few weeks, a number of independent groups occupied a public building in the market square recently, and got the right to rooms of their own.

There is Krakow WIP, dominated by Stazcek and Radoslaw Huget, an ex-KPN man, who last night was arguing for direct action to change the street sign saying July 22nd. Manifestation to Pilsudski Street. This was vetoed by everyone else, as they didn't see why a peace and freedom movement should make propaganda for Pilsudski, who was a soldier. They did agree to another "Troops out" action on the November 7th outside the Soviet consulate. Krakow WIP has seceded from the rest of the WIP federation because it doesn't agree with "structure." It is now busy helping to organise an independent Trade Union for Conscientious objectors.

Krakow NZS has also seceded from the national NZS because it doesn't agree that only the praesidium can act in the name of NZS. It wants each university to be able to act autonomously. (Something that was possble in the 1980–81 period.) Gregorsz

Surdy, a student at the Jagellonian university, felt it was Geremek and Solidarity influence pushing for a centralized structure as this meant "more control," less conflict from students. Krakow WIP also support the independent Student Boycott committee, who held an organising meeting today. Over fifty universities are now involved, nationwide, with the boycott of military classes, 100% effective in most places. Even so the committee was anxious at NZS, the main one, giving in too easily over their heads, and was discussing occupation of the military studies department as the next tactic. The Art and Music students did not agree. They felt one should "go for what's possible."

And there are Greens: the Polish Ecological Club, Green federation, and various bits of Green Party whose complex internal feuds Tomas tried explaining last week.

The drama of the various feuds and intensity of activity, perhaps compensates for the small numbers involved. Very few women, possibly they have more sense, or simply dislike the aggressive confrontational style. I certainly come away feeling slightly exhausted and understanding absolutely, why another friend, Bogdan Klich says that these days he is staying outside "the political game."

Bogdan's life in the last ten years reads like a short course in opposition politics in Poland. He flirted with nationalism in his teens, drawn by the romance of KPN's conspiratorial politics and then in 1980, as a medical student threw himself into the newly formed WZS. The work was so exhausting, especially the last months of a student strike that internment, and Martial law was almost a relief. He feigned appendicitis, undergoing the operation to avoid a more punitive prison sentence (for singing in his cell) and was released after nine months. Then followed the years of growing disillusion as society appeared increasingly apathetic; joining WIP in 1986 because it seemed to offer "the opportunity to be active again"; getting reinvolved in the strikes in May 1988 and supporting the Round table and elections as they occurred. Now he felt "unsure of his place." "I hoped the Round table would in some sense open up society. But actually it was an agreement between political forces, not people and those forces: church, Solidarity, Party, still predetermine the divisions in the rest of society. In one sense citizens weren't included. I'm not saying Solidarity doesn't represent the majority, it does. The problem is that it loses minorities – those other people, groups who also 'belong'.

Democracy is about including minorities." Not that he saw those numerous small organisations as a real force in society. "There's no civil society in Poland. In the early eighties civil society was organised around Solidarity, but as years went by less and less people were engaged. The Trade Union and political structure were renewed, not civil society. The new government doesn't see that most people simply stay on the outside, unengaged politically, going abroad to work, and not even feeling responsible for their own lives. Take our staircase for example," he remarked in sudden irritation, "no one in this building feels responsible for cleaning it."

A thoughtful, introspective man looking older than his 29 years, he lives with his parents, sharing a room with his five year old son Matheus. He was preoccupied at the moment with trying to get the magazine he had founded, *Tumult*, registered. Registration means a wider distribution in kiosks. It is also a costly and complex process.

The magazine, a combination of political discussion and culture, was his solution to staying outside "the game" yet speaking to it. He showed me with pride his article arguing strongly with a recent statement by a prominent artist that "now is the time for politics, culture should be silent. All our forces are needed in the battle and we should not preoccupy ourselves with other affairs."

"There is always a conflict of loyalties though," he said. "Solidarity in a sense is my emotional home, so it's hard to criticize."

Sunday October 29th
Krakow

Mark is here, doing his half of the **Rough Guide to Poland**, with little support from Polorbis, who are not too keen on the Rough guides concept of travel. He persuaded me to abandon politics yesterday afternoon and go and look at an exhibition: "Jews in Poland." The organisers have clearly decided to gather together every picture about Jewish life they could find and simply hang them on the walls. This makes it interesting but hard to absorb. Still the exhibition was packed. There is definitely an increasing interest in Judaism in Poland, not just in intellectual, former opposition circles but within the catholic church itself, beginning many years ago with articles and seminars, an Episcopal Commission for Dialogue with Judaism. The Carmelite convent controversy demonstrated however, that anti-semitism is alive and well. Perhaps, inevitably, the revived interest and revived antagonism go hand in hand. Some Polish intellectuals published a thoughtful letter last month saying, "The intention of the Carmelite nuns to pray on the site of genocide is noble and beautiful: its goal was not to divide the nation. If however, its result turned out to be to deepen divisions and not rapprochement one must withdraw without looking for those guilty. Many irresponsible embittering arguments . . . were used on both sides under the impact of emotions. It is time to stop them . . . The best solution would be . . . the ideas agreed in the Geneva accord (to remove the convent outside the camp and establish an inter-religious prayer centre)". Cardinal Glemp has said he intends to implement the accord, but the fall out from his earlier remarks, accusing Jews of "infringing hard won sovereignty," having the mass media at their disposal, continues. David Warzawski, now Kostek Gebert, an eminent journalist, active in Solidarity opposition and both Polish and Jewish, wrote an article about Glemp's remarks saying "Now in Poland, I feel a bit less at home." *Tygodnik Solidarnosc*, the Solidarity weekly felt it was "too emotional" and counterproductive and so refused to publish. He put it in the reformist Communist weekly *Polityka* (for the first time in his life) and, while getting a lot of private support had little from the public. One letter reminded him of the role the Jews played under Stalin, saying "after these experiences we want no more Jews." He described all this in another thoughtful article pointing out that "until now Poles have had no way to freely sort out their history, their attitudes to others, to strike a moral balance." He sees Glemp's attack as a second battle "after unsuccessful church sponsored anti-abortion campaign against the non-clerical, non-natonalistic, antiauthoritarian current in the Polish opposition." Glemp would, he feels, give strong support to a Christian Democratic party continuing the prewar "anti-semitic," "nationalist," "National Democratic" tradition.

"Catholic elites and Solidarity leadership have countered these drives," he concludes. Certainly my own experience so far is that most people point out "the dangers" of these tendencies. I have yet to meet someone who actually supports them.

Outside the museum Mark and I got talking to a visiting Israeli Jew. He felt the problem was not so much anti-semitism as a certain ignorance and insensitivity.

"It's extraordinary – you go to a town – one of the most important places for Hassidic Jews for example, and the Yeshiva is a furniture store, no one knows it exists. Or like our guide, a very nice person, who tries to explain Talmudic discussion by likening it to a discussion among Christ's disciples. She has no idea that this might offend." He told us that on one occasion an old man had walked up to the group and started angrily telling them off for teaching young Israelis, that Poles were anti-semitic. All the same he was glad to have come.

The conversation reminded me of another friend's experience at Auschwitz. Listening to a guide explain who had died there, he noticed she made no mention of Jews, just total numbers. When he challenged her on this, she looked surprised and said, but of course, if she was showing Jews around, she would mention Jews.

Apparently there is now a cafeteria serving creamcakes. This too leaves me feeling distinctly uncomfortable. Auschwitz is not a theme park or a motor museum. You don't put tea shops in cemeteries.

"Well," Neil said cynically when he heard it, "it means you can now have near enough the complete concentration camp experience. See the exhibition and try to understand what it felt like to be a victim, and then have tea and see what it felt like to run the place."

Monday October 30th
Warsaw

I got home last night to find the political axis tilted a few more degrees. A Warsaw pact meeting ended last week with an agreement that every nation could determine its own future without external interference. No one talked about leaving the pact, just of altering the way it functions, but then today the Kremlin announced that Hungary could leave if it wanted. In Poland "the withdrawal of Soviet troops depends on both alliances," but according to Deputy foreign Minister Kulski "it may not be long before the need to station Soviet troops in Poland ceases to exist."

Meanwhile Polish demonstrators have been arrested on an enormous demonstraton in Prague, with yet more predictable, police violence. There are about 1500 East Germans in the West German embassy and Poles are applying for work permits to go and live in GDR. Ironically, housing and job prospects are better there.

Wednesday November 1st
Poznan

Zosia told me to "go and find a graveyard, it's very beautiful." Today is the day Polish people remember their dead. Elzbieta, the friend with whom I am staying, told me that when she was a child she and her family would spend the previous three days cleaning the grave. Now they just visit on the day, and she has gone off accordingly with her mother. I, family-less, went round the corner to the local cemetery. And it was beautiful, a mass of candle light, everywhere, and chrysanthemums; graves neatly gardened; families in their best clothes, sometimes three, sometimes four generations. It felt like Christmas without the presents. I helped a solitary, elderly lady having difficulty with her candle, then came home. Later Elzbieta came back from her own dead and we took flowers and candles to the Monument commemorating the demonstrations of 1956. The heavy concrete crosses are imposing rather than beautiful and the statue of Mickiewicz must be the ugliest ever; a sort of Balzac by Rodin pose, but *no* grace. However in the flickering candlelight it had a certain presence. "The police used to encircle this place," Elzbieta remarked, "it was a kind of game to beat them and make as long a cross of candles as possible." Some people had made a small memorial to the Victims of Tianamen.

Somehow, when we got back, we got on to a discussion of "Shoah." Elzbieta asked me if I thought it was fair. I couldn't answer. "Fairness" didn't seem to me what it was about. The film presented with extraordinary power what happened to Jews in Poland and how some Germans and Poles behaved, some of them with honour and dignity. Nothing can be the "whole truth." There is surely more to say and this film doesn't preclude it. I do not know how one can approach genocide in a "balanced way." "I wish," she said "we could just start from now! To say to Jewish people we don't feel like that. Things are different." It sounded sensible, but thinking about it now, as I write, I can't agree. It's not enough. This country of all places is somewhere where the dead are not forgotten and history counts.

The bookshops and papers at the moment are full of articles about Katyn and the thousands murdered by the communists between 1945 and the early fifties, rightly so. I find myself agreeing with Cardnal Glemp when he said at a Mass last week "there is no desire for revenge, but one has a duty to discover the whole truth concerning the past." That's why failing to put up plaques on furniture stores that were once Yeshivas or to mention the numbers of Jews killed in Auschwitz is so important. You need to know about the past to have any sense of the future. Silence is the worst thing, it means: nothing. Elzbieta asked me how Jewish I was. Jewish enough to be dead in another time and place, and it does matter.

Thursday November 2nd
Poznan

"Bother Lech Walesa, I could kill him!" Elzbieta announced this evening as we were washing up. His crime is that he recently made a speech, speaking in favour of Zarnowiec. "I've just decided not to be active and then this happens. I don't want to go to the demonstration tomorrow. There will only be 10 people, we'll have to get up at 5 a.m. Must I go?" I couldn't answer this, I don't much like early starts myself but as the Ministry of Industry were meeting to make up their minds on whether to contnue Zarnowiec or not, a demonstration might have some point.

Elzbieta Olezka is a striking woman wth red hair and green eyes and a quirky sense of humour. She lectures in sociology at Poznan University, and is doing her PhD on ecological movements. She had been involved in oppositional activities since 1980, particularly in ecological actions in the last three years but now wanted to withdraw and concentrate on academic work. "I feel uncertain about what's going on, I can't grasp what's happening completely." The phrases are beginning to sound familiar. "Solidarity is the framework for all group activity now and it's hard to work outside it. In Wroclaw that's fine. WIP were invited to be on the Citizens' Committee. Its leading members are in Solidarity, Radek stood as a deputy. Here in Poznan relationships are not so good. We were not invited to join. "They see WIP as young, radical, direct action." In fact Poznan WIP are mainly a group of Sociologists – university teachers and students who spend as much time organising seminars as doing actions. "And they've simply transferred all the old mechanisms of the opposition to government level. If you were a friend of Kuron before, you are now. They asked me, through Radek, to run an environmental foundation. I rejected it. I don't like fund raising, I don't like that kind of politics, every decision having to be pushed through every level of the hierarchy. So I've missed my opportunity to join the establishment." She pulled a face.

"Actually I find Polish society quite frightening in some ways. You know, people wanted Mazowiecki on television once a week to say what he was doing, to control him, they couldn't just trust him. I don't like 'Direct Democracy'."

"But you like WIP taking direct action."

"That's different, it's thought out, consciously, we meet, educate ourselves, read. There's a difference between that and action taken by unconscious 'masses', open to manipulation. That's dangerous." She thought for a bit.

"Perhaps ecology is different, it requires spontaneous action. People need to act because they are frightened. Anyway I hate the words direct action, too abused by the Communists." She mused some more, "perhaps I just think I'm an anarchist and I'm really an 'elitist'. Deep down I fear 'lack of control'."

Friday November 3rd
Warsaw

We made the early morning train, Elzbieta prowling round the apartment at 5 a.m. in stretch tights and T-shirt saying it felt like suicide. "And you can be sure whatever train compartment we are in will be completely full, even if the rest of the train is empty!" She was right, but we found an empty first class compartment and promptly went to sleep.

In Warsaw, Elzbieta insisted on coffee in a grim looking cafe opposite the Forum Hotel. "This place is very special," she said. "The decor hasn't changed since the fifties. And all the waitresses are very old and sweet, it's like having tea with your Aunt." I looked round again: high ceiling with white oval discs suspended from it in which orange, plastic, ball shaped light fittings were placed giving a sputnik effect, high glass counter, juke box in corner and yes elderly waitress in starched white pinafores. However it still seemed unredeemably ugly to me. But there you are – Stalinist decor now has cult value.

Outside the Ministry of Industry the banners outnumbered the demonstrators. "Zarnowiec, the window on another world," "New government, old mistakes." Jaremar Dubiel, a friend from Sopot, said he had hoped for 2000, but Walesa could take society with him on the issue. He felt it was all to do with the sudden "gift" of 600 million dollars of emergency aid announced by the French government. "They want to sell their nuclear technology, don't they? I expect Giscard D'Estaing discussed it with Lech Walesa. I hoped this issue could pull the ecological movement together."

It was very cold, more people arrived including a bunch of banner waving, trumpet blowing schoolchildren and their "leader," a longhaired byronic looking man, in a long black coat whom everyone called Belfer (a Polish word for "teacher"). The group was called Twe Twa and they had been picketing the Council of ministers for three days.

By 1 p.m. it was quite a large crowd: young punks, older men with longish hair and beards, some university teachers, students, a secret policeman. A man called Gregorz Pesco from Krakow lectured me on the politics of the Green Federation: Ecology wasn't a set of isolated problems connected with environmental degradation, it was a holistic approach to life admiring its richness and biological and social diversity. Communism was the most "abscessed face of industrial civilisation but we don't want to get stuck with the problems of highly industrialised market economies either! There are values that can't be translated into money. The trouble is," he said gloomily, "even Mazowiecki has said he is in favour of nuclear energy. It's not a good time to be challenging the basic ideology of liberalism and industrial growth. To say one can be happy without having 'more' sounds very strange."

Staszek and Belfer made speeches through a hand held speaker. A French MEP said she hoped the Poles would be more successful than the French. Then everyone spontaneously decided to go into the meeting and just picked up their banners, walked past the doorman who didn't complain, up the stairs and with a peremptory knock, into the meeting room. The men sitting around the oval table with bottles of mineral water and papers, seemed quite unperturbed by some seventy assorted activists and an almost equal number of banners, including one whose poles sported two skulls, encircling them. The chairman politely stood up. "A very stupid man," Elzbieta muttered in my ear. Belfer made a speech and handed over a petition. Another man stood up and said "Thank you, now please go away so we can continue our work. Let me assure you I'm against nuclear power, but I can argue better without you here."

"Bogarski," Elzbieta muttered again, "definitely against." Bogarski promised to came out at 3 p.m. and announce the result and after a few more murmurs from protestors about Chernobyl, we all filed out and down the stairs. I was completely astonished, trying to imagine a similar scene at home. We wouldn't get past the security guard.

By 3 p.m. it was clear no decision had been made and the demonstration marched up Nowy Swit to the prime minister's residence. When Elzbieta and I ran for our train, Staszek was suggesting they should go in there as well.

Saturday November 4th
Poznan

Today I participated in a "historical event." This was how Elzbieta's friend, Baszia described Poland's first national, feminist conference. The Poznan Women's Club had invited women's groups from all over the country to get together and share ideas. Baszia, who found Poland so sexist, she had moved to Amsterdam, had returned especially for the occasion.

Three men and about fifty women, mostly professionals in their twenties and thirties had gathered in a small seminar room. The men were a surprise to me, also to Baszia. "How can a feminist group be 30% men," she had asked as a stocky man from an organisation called "Profemina" introduced himself, as their representative.

"We don't use the word feminism," a woman from the same

group replied. "Our priority is to fight for women's right to conscious motherhood."

"You implied in the article you wrote in *Polityka* you were only a women's group," a journalist from Krakow said sharply, "you should have made it clear."

"And what has anticlericalism got to do with feminism?" a dark haired woman asked a smartly dressed, moustached man from the "Anticlericalist League." "We're against the church hierarchy, you should support an antichurch movement because there are quite a number of national organisations forming now, that will organise against you." He had an aggressive, sharp manner that contrasted with the women's more tentative approach and having along with the other men placed himself squarely in the front rows, now had to turn awkwardly to speak to the women behind him.

"But we want to go in quite a different direction; we want the pope to be our friend," the woman said.

"We're not against religion, we're trying to interfere inside the church," he replied.

"Sounds like the Ministry of Interior to me, it's up to the church to decide its own way of organising," another woman said.

The discussion moved on to other familiar topics: whether to organise a women's political party or not: yes, "because we want influence;" no, "because we don't want either sex ruling the other;" "our main concern is to raise consciousness, we need a socialist movement not a party;" whether to work separately from men or not: no, "because issues like ecology affect us all, we need to change men;" yes, "because working separately is the only situation in which we can understand the stereotypes that oppress us;" how to propagate "another model for women's lives apart from that available in traditional Polish family life."

At lunch time two women from "the Women's League" arrived, saying that a radio announcer that morning had expressed anxiety at the conference "degenerating into gossip." It showed no danger of doing so. There were talks on patriarchy, pacifism, the silence about women in Polish history and philosophy.

By tea time however the man from Profemina was feeling frustrated. First of all he felt he had not had as much time to discuss his views as other women and secondly, women were being very impractical, failing to discuss "concrete proposals" like "bulletins," "campaigns." "Don't treat us instrumentally," Elzbieta responded.

"First we simply want to find out how each of us feels about things."

She wanted to know about "the Women's League." Gosza, in Gdansk had also expressed anxiety about the Women's League, organised by the Communist Party after the second World War "in order to appear progressive." "They had no independent political influence at all. Their main activity was to organise excursions to places where one could buy otherwise unavailable consumer goods." Gosza was concerned that, recognising women as a political force, they would make use of this to revitalise their own organisation. Profemina, for example was heavily influenced by the Women's League. "Women don't understand that Profemina is not an authentic women's organisation at all, men take all the decisions."

Now Elzbieta was asking, "Are you here just looking for support for the Women's League or are you reforming yourselves?" The Women's League women looked very friendly if somewhat different from the other more casually dressed women. One was plump with dyed blonde curls, false eyelashes, and synthetic leopard skin top, tightly belted with white plastic belt over short tight skirt. The other in contrast, had short gray hair in a masculine cut, wore a T-shirt saying Fanatic and workman's trousers. "We want to take the Women's league where it has never gone before," the blonde woman said sounding rather like captain Kirk on the Starship Enterprise. They were reforming themselves, of course it would be easier if more feminists came into the organisation. Moreover in the struggle to protect women's right to abortion, unity was needed. Darek, one of the men agreed. "We should ignore our differences and work on this urgent issue together."

"It might be politically necessary," Suzanna from PPS-RD argued. "This feminist association is very elitist and the Women's League has a representative in every factory. They could activate working women."

"Could they," said a woman called Magda, "after forty years of doing nothing? Who will listen?"

"I don't want to collaborate with an organisation with which I have only one point in common and differ in everything else," said Elzbieta. The Women's League woman shifted her ground. "We're not so much feminists, we have a Christian approach," she said, somewhat surprisingly, "Most Polish women go to church and won't enter a feminist movement." "It's not a question of making all women 'active feminists' but making sure they have a right to choose their own way of life," another woman replied.

At this point positions became rather confused. Darek and the man from the Anticlericalist League pointing out that the church was "a military organisation that required a militant struggle to combat it." Elzbieta responded that while she had problems with the church she was a Christian and she thought Darek sounded like a Stalinist. "It's utterly mistaken to attack it this way."

"The church is a political institution that needs to be dealt with politically," said Suzanna firmly.

"But you can't ignore the fact that it provides a social and moral context for people's lives, particularly Polish women," responded Elzbieta sounding suddenly rather like the women from the Women's League.

"Enough," Baszia called, "time to go." The man from the anticlericalist group wasn't happy, he wanted the last word: "You feminists will never succeed in Poland if you don't join us! Why? Because you are against Patriarchy, that is your problem."

Western stereotypes simply do not apply in Poland, not just because words like left, right, socialist, feminist, catholic don't match their Western counterparts but because they don't describe unitary phenomena. It's hard for example as a woman to get to grips with a church that seems to both liberate and oppress. Providing on the one hand essential physical and intellectual space for the opposition in its buildings and publications,supporting pacifists, reaching out in dialogue to the Jews, and on the other, also appearing to support militant, nationalist, sometimes racist thinking. On the abortion issue it has made things very simple – it is not a question of a woman's right to make autonomous decisions regarding her body; the foetus is a human being from the word go. Abortion is murder, full stop.

I have catholic, pacifist friends in Torun WIP who with logical consistency combine campaigns against abortion with those against militarism and violence. They also believe that "tolerance is the foundation of a free people" and therefore quite happily coexist in a network with "proabortion" activists.

When we got home, exhausted, Elzbieta turned on the radio: 200,000 people demonstrating in the GDR. The biggest demonstration so far, demanding free elections and better travel laws.

There is a Polish Czech solidarity meeting going on in Wroclaw and thousands of Czechs have been stopped trying to cross the border to attend. Thousands have also succeeded, by travelling to Poland through East Germany. The Czech embassy denied any knowledge of events at the Polish border.

The radio went on to report the break in to the PPS flat in Wspolna. Suzanna had told us this morning that, on Friday evening, after the Zarnowiec demonstration, a group of men with sticks had beaten up two women who opened the door to them. One was still in hospital. Staszek, who was there and others from Krakow WIP ran after them and caught two of them. The radio was now reporting that these were both 17 years old and from "good" schools. They told the police that they had gone to that flat because "they had heard Communists were there." The police are investigating. "Welcome to democratic politics," Suzanna had said this morning. Elzbieta was pacing around the room.

"Sometimes," she said "I just can't stand facing this 'very historical moment in Poland'. I'm fed up with it. I would like to live in a boring country where the radio talks about boring problems!"

Sunday November 5th
Wroclaw

Elzbieta was not so fed up with historical moments that she didn't want us both to skip the discussion on natural childbirth and ecofeminism and got another 5.30 a.m. train to Wroclaw to meet the Czechs and go to a seminar "Central Europe in Tumult: between Totalitarianism and Commercialism."

"You missed the best bit!" Jan Kavan (from Palach Press in London) told me when we arrived. He was almost dancing on the spot with glee. "Just incredible, Kryl and Huta playing in the Teatr Polski, 6000 young Czechs shouting 'Long live Havel', they wouldn't let him stop. I thought they were going to march out of the theatre and start the revolution immediately, in Wroclaw."

In the lecture theatre, the Czechs, serious young people in denims and leather jackets were listening to Ivan Svitak discuss the problems of a common European Home. "Are we going to have a closed elitist society? What about Bulgarians, Estonians, Lithuanians, Ukrainians? What about 'gast arbeiter'? The Communists screened people according to class origin. Wll we do it according to geography?" Another historian stressed the problems of difficulties between peoples; the Polish Hungarian cooperation against Czechoslovakia before the war; Polish: Lithuanian, Hungarian: Rumanian antagonisms. Jiri Pelikan suggested that 'each nation should build its own house first and perhaps later look for the common roof, and also emphasised the need not to forget social justice.' Many Poles are crossing the Czech border to buy bread and butter which Polish Democracy does not guarantee them."

It felt a little different from the previous day, sitting in a beautiful baroque hall with the plaster forms of a variety of philosophers staring down at us. Whatever else happens it is clear that our future "Common European Home" will be run by men, at least at the outset. I'm not very tolerant of long speeches. I listened to a moving letter from the Czech philosopher Simecka saying his utopia was quite modest: "not a market economy, but just the ability to attend a meeting with friends without wondering how many policemen were around, or to be able to take a slow, second class train to Wroclaw." Then I walked around in the cobbled streets, watched Czechs queuing to get into a small second hand bookshop, bumped into Radek who was bubbling over at having a new daughter, in perfect health; and came back into the lobby where Adam Michnik was having an emotional argument with a Russian who wanted Christianity and to hang all the Communists. "The only way to democracy is compromise, look at Spain," Adam Michnik said. "I would put their names in the paper, announce their guilt, try to pay back the humiliation they caused. It's not a question of those who win against those who lose. Did Nuremberg stop anyone?" He took up the theme again that evening in a final speech. "When I hear the call for another Nuremberg process, I warn you, from the perspective of a man who has been a prisoner. Those who know the taste of prison bread and have heard the voice of a prison officer don't wish the same on anyone, even their enemies." And he went on to speak to the Czechs about Poland's part in the invasion of 1968. "I must say that we are guilty, and we should not try to find historical justifications for our presence in the guilt. I repeat once again what we have been repeating since 1968. Yes, we are guilty and we are very sorry."

"We are a frustrated country," a Czech man said at the press conference. "We have the strongest democratic tradition and now we are the last to change. We have no tradition of open revolt, but we would make the most of democracy if we had it."

On the train back to Warsaw I asked Jan Kavan what he would do if the situation changed. "Give me twenty minutes to pack my bags," he replied.

Monday November 6th
Warsaw

Financial speculation is not my forte. I would be useless in the City. The dollar was falling all last week (7000 zloties at the beginning, 6000 at the end) and I avoided changing money in the foolish belief that it might rise again. This evening the rather sinister looking men outside the National Bank offered 5,500 and "it will be less tomorrow," they said threateningly, while at the change office in the pedestrian passage ways under Marszalkowska it was 5,800. It pays to shop around. The dilemma of course is whether to change all the money I need to live on, now, in case it keeps falling, or hold out in hope.

I understand enough economics to know this is a good for Poland of course. Zosza tells me it is all thanks to two philanthropic Polish millionaires who decided to put loads of dollars on the market, forcing the free rate down while Balcerowicz is devaluing the zloty and bringing the oficial rate up, thus bringing a convertible zloty that much nearer. And of course the process has escalated, as everyone is dumping their dollars in the hope of buying them back later at a cheaper rate. Bogdan however sees the rate of the dollar as a good indicator of general mood. A high rate indicates uncertainty and pessimism, a low rate stability and hope.

Tuesday November 7th
Warsaw

People must be getting increasingly hopeful. The dollar is still falling – 5,200 or 5,600 depending where you look. Friends say it won't rise again before Christmas so I've changed all I need, and feel virtuous at the thought of contributing to Poland's economic renewal.

Kostek Gebert was back from the "What's Left" conference in

Florence and had mail from T. so I went round to his flat. T. is now in Slovenia tied up with the ZSMS Congress. They have just decided to turn themselves into a political party and run in Slovenia's first multiparty elections. ZSMS actually stands for "Alliance of Socialist Youth of Slovenia" but having transformed themselves from junior wing of the Communist Party, to umbrella group for social movements, to oppositional party, they have decided the "S" now stands for liberty (Svoboda) not Socialism.

Kostek tells me he handed round a questionnaire in Florence: "Socialism is a Bloody Waste of Time: Agree, Disagree?" All the East Europeans: Miklos Harasti from Budapest, T., Kostek, Pavel Bratinka from Czechoslovakia, except Boris Kagarlitsky from the Soviet Union, agreed. All the Western Leftists disagreed.

Kostek thinks Poland is heading to social revolt. "People feel betrayed. What started as a movement of ten million people ended as a compromise between elites. The choice was to negotiate with illegitimate authority or sit it out, hoping that authority would be swept away by the Winds of History. The Solidarity leadership didn't want that anyway, because of the side effects. Surprisingly, so far, negotiation has worked, I don't think it can in the long run. A substantial part of this population is not going to continue to accept a contract made up in their name but behind their backs. They wanted a free country, what they got is free prices," he said, quoting one of his own articles.

He saw the root of the problem as the "nomenclatura." "It's a criminal mafia, who are actively working to destroy this country. A free market makes no sense unless their backbone is broken, nor will this government get real political support. The demise of the nomenclatura means the demise of Communism." He didn't feel the government were doing enough. "Their power base is at local level. The central nomenclatura is competent and secure, but locally, it's corrupt and inefficient. They could be sacked overnight." The solution was to have proper local elections as soon as possible. Then "give the local authorities final say in the authorisation of private enterprise, allow them to clamp down on ecological problems, give them control of the local police (who still regularly beat people up); and the situation would change overnight, without spending a cent or involving the IMF."

It was rather similar to what Leshek Budrewicz, chief information officer for Solidarity Trade Union in Wroclaw, had been saying to me two days earlier. He too felt people needed something more concrete than just being told the economic changes were necessary." They can't keep repeating "it will get better" when for 30%, mostly young people, it's going to be a catastrophe. Kuron just offering free soup makes people laugh. We know the economic situation is terrible but if you can't give bread at least show people that something has really changed. Leshek's solutions were: don't have Mazowiecki on TV looking just like the Communists, shaking people's hands, flowers from children and so on, have him arguing, discussing things; don't put privatised industry straight into the hands of the nomenclatura just because they have money and it avoids conflict; and have the local elections in spring, not autumn as Lech Walesa was suggesting.

"They couldn't reach agreement on this issue at the Round Table and the question is now, where is the greatest danger?" Kostek continued. "Do you compromise with the Communists on this, to get other reforms, provoke a few idiots in Krakow and hope people's endurance holds out? Or do you tackle the Communists head on like John Wayne? In my opinion the first option is bullshit. The second," he shrugged, "the Peasants and Democrats could obstruct and bring the government down – so we would have open conflict and polarisation on both sides. But if we are going to have a social explosion anyway – the question is which side of the barricades do we want to be on?"

Kostek, as David Warzawski, was instrumental in KOS (an underground opposition network called the Committee for Social Resistance) in opening up a dialogue with the Western Peace movement and in particular END (European Nuclear Disarmament) in the early eighties. Strange to sit talking with someone to whom you have been writing anonymously for years.

I had to run to dinner. Mark has finished his Rough Guide and leaves tomorrow, so we went out to eat with Piotr C. and Marek Kosakowski. Marek's girlfriend, also a journalist on the foreign desk of Gazeta Wyborcza, arrived excited and late. Excited because she had just received a grant from Mrs Thatchers KnowHow fund for journalists, to work on *The Guardian* and late because she had had to rewrite the front page. "They wanted an article on the GDR. And there really was nothing *new*, except more demonstrations. Then just as I'd finished we heard, the whole government has resigned!"

Friday November 10th
Warsaw

Zosia rang me this morning in a state of great excitement.

"They're taking down the Berlin Wall!"

"What do you mean taking it down, who? Demonstrators?" It was still quite early for me and I felt confused.

"No, the Government! They've opened the gates, and in Bonn everyone stood up in parliament and embraced and Gorbachev has said it's all right and Zivkov has resigned."

"Zivkov?" Zosia was talking very fast and I was finding it hard to absorb.

"Zivkov, Party chief in Bulgaria. Kohl has asked Mazowiecki if he can go home." (Kohl is here along with the half the world's media on a visit of historic importance.) "Isn't it shocking?"

"Shocking? Well I think it's amazing."

"Shocking and amazing," she agreed, insisting before hanging up that I come round to watch Sky television in the evening.

I looked out of the window. Everything looked the same. People going in and out of the vegetable shop, a queue at the kiosk on the corner, spiky bedraggled trees and "The Crass" scrawled in white paint on the opposite walls. I still couldn't quite grasp the fact that the physical and political reality that has shaped my world for all of my life and dominated it for the last ten years is suddenly crumbling away. "Perhaps now I can go back to East Germany." This thought seemed rather trivial compared with the enormity of the event, but it preoccupied me. The last time I tried in 1983 they took me off the train to Poland and sent me back to Friedrichstrasse, END being rather unpopular in the GDR at that time.

This evening I sat with Zosia and her husband Sigismund, just back from working in West Germany, and watched euphoric Berliners drinking champagne astride the wall and endless documentary footage: the airlift, barbed wire, Kennedy speaking, people being shot, digging tunnels, more barbed wire – the ugliness and stupidity of it all.

Zosia told me that when she watched them stand up in the parliament in Bonn and sing the National anthem she did have a sudden moment of anxiety. "You see," she said almost apologetically, "we remember the war." The government spokeswoman Niezabitoswka was on television, impassive as ever, saying "Poles welcome the event but the permanency of current borders must be guaranteed," and that "a new united Germany should not threaten European security."

When I got home there was a woman standing at the bottom of the stairs, clutching the banisters as if she was drowning. Dirty hair, dirty face, a cut above her eyebrow and blood on her cheap white anorak, she swayed from side to side, weeping. When I tried to ask if she was all right (stupid question) or lived here, she mumbled incoherently and burst into yet more noisy tears. I see drunks every day in Poland, cursing in the street or lying asleep in the subway passages. I manage to hurry by, turning my head away, feeling useless, but this woman was on my staircase . . . My Polish wasn't good enough to help her alone, besides she was very big. I banged on a door. A man opened it, looked at the woman, looked at me in amazement and shut it quickly. After banging on two more with no response, I managed to persuade the woman to at least sit down and ran up the stairs to my own apartment to ring Zosia. "We'll come at once," she said. At the botom of the stairs the woman was now a crumpled heap. Two men came down. The first stepped over her, smiled at me and said something like "don't be stupid, she's drunk," and I, suddenly incensed, shouted after him in English "maybe that's how you treat drunks here but not in my country!" (What nonsense! and where such national chauvinism springs from in me, I can't think.) The second man, a big, burly, kindly faced one, helped me get the woman on her feet and up the stairs to my apartment. This wasn't easy as her trousers kept falling down and her insistence on pinning her knees together to keep them up, made it hard for her to walk.

Once indoors she seemed to recover a little. She asked for water, refused bread and cheese and covered my hand with kisses, sitting awkwardly in the upholstered chair. I went through her white, plastic handbag looking for an address. It contained a half eaten doughnut, a bottle of antibiotics, two torn fragments of photograph: a young man and a young woman, and her identity card; no keys, no money. Zosia and Sigismund arrived. I could tell Sigismund didn't altogether approve, as he was quite gruff, though kindly. "We'll take her home, it's quite near," Zosia decided, "some people get the police, but they are too brutal." It took sometime, what with the trousers, the continued weeping, and the fact that she couldn't remember the entrance to her apartment building. Halfway up the final flight of stairs with Sigismund already banging on her door, she froze, burying her head in my shoulder as Zosia and I propped her up, refusing to go further. The young man from the photo, now in a bathrobe, opened the door. He stared angrily at the woman, grasped her arm and she went, head hanging, meekly up beside him. He thanked us very politely and the door closed, "I wonder how often that happens," Zosia said. "I wonder what misery goes on inside," I remarked.

Sunday November 12th
Warsaw

Every house has a Polish flag flying, still up from yesterday. November 11th has a special meaning here, celebrating the birth of an independent Poland in 1918. "And an official holiday for the first time," Zosia says happily, "unfortunately on a Saturday, but never mind."

It is Pilsudski's day of course. We have had nonstop commemorative programmes on televsion and my bookshop window on the corner is a virtual shrine. There are six different books on Pilsudski including one by the man himself, four books on Katyn, two on the Warsaw uprising, plus other assorted titles – Dmowski: Polish Politics and the Formation of the State; Days of Struggle in the Capital; The Disappeared in the Soviet Union; A History of the Sejm; Diplomacy 1939; The 58th Infantry Company of the Great Polish Nation. In the record section the Polish legionnaires have ousted Linda Rondstadt and Marilyn Monroe. And stuck to the wall is a KPN poster inviting me to yesterday's celebration mass.

I share Elzbieta's feeling of sometmes being a little buffeted by history, gusting and blowing around me and now shifting under my feet. Everything resonates with everything else – old fights replayed: Nationalists demonstrate against Communists and on occasion try to beat them up. As before the war, there are now at least three peasant parties and two Polish Socialist Parties. Apart from the Communists these groups play minor roles at present, but it is as if they were determined to summon up old ghosts and old animosities.

And now of course just as they celebrate their own "reunification" Poles see the continent reshaping itself in the old mould.

Everyone seems to simply assume the reunification of Germany will occur. This, in spite of Gerasimov, Foreign Affairs spokesman for the Soviet government, saying that the Soviet Union will not tolerate tampering with the boundaries of the Warsaw Pact.

"Germany is a problem for us," Krysza remarked, having made supper for me tonight. "We now have a completely new neighbour – we don't know what will happen."

My Warsaw feminist friends however appear not to be haunted. They held their "pro choice" demonstration outside the U.S. embassy. The NZS refused to support it, not because it didn't support the issue, but because it felt it was wrong to protest here, but about 70 people including quite a few babies, turned up and they made the TV news.

Monday November 13th
Warsaw

T. is back from Slovenia. Zosia asked us to come and talk English to her economics students so we sat in an enchoing classroom and discussed the current state of affairs. Some of them had been taught by Balcerowicz the previous term and assured us he was practising what he preached. Not that they agreed with it all, raising yet again the problem of the nomenclatura. "They are the ones with enough money to be major shareholders in a newly privatised industry. People won't work more efficiently just to see all the profit go to an unpopular old boss and not to the state. And there's no law to say that former directors can't be shareholders." "And if workers buy shares at 10% of their yearly income it will take 120 years for them to buy all the property." "I think workers should just be given shares."

Kostek Gebert told me that he thought in some ways the old opposition structure of Solidarity was "Anti-young." "It had to be to survive underground. And that lost us a generation." Listening to these students I felt that in one sense he might be right. Only two people in the class were actively engaged in politics: one in NZS, and another in his local Citizens committee. They both insisted that it was "impossible to be outside politics everyone is interested" and that "lots of young people helped in the elections." The others however did not seem interested. They were glad to have a "wise government," that had their confidence and didn't even seem perturbed at the suggestion from one student that a new Solidarity Party was "monopolizing the media just like the Communists had done."

"The question of who govern is of no importance as long as people have food," one said surprisingly. "Pluralism is beside the point when we have an economic crisis."

Their main concern was to find their own places to live. "We have been building Socialism for 45 years and it still takes twenty years to find a flat. Under capitalism it may take twelve." Meanwhile they wanted to go into business. One of them was running her own shop already.

The market value of the dollar has risen again: 10,000 on Friday, 7,000 today. Janek laughed when I told him about my efforts at prediction. "Should have asked me," he said.

Tuesday November 14th
Warsaw

Chancellor Kohl came back and has left again, having embraced Marzowiecki, and promised that the Federal Republic of Germany will respect Poland's western border, although he can't speak for "the whole of Germany." So in spite of substantial amounts of economic aid, no one is completely reassured. Sosia's students yesterday felt Kohl's calls for a united Europe "just a manipulation – it would be more profitable for them to have a larger market."

"We're indoctrinated," one of them confessed, "we have all grown up after the war being told all the time about this very bad, very strong Germany. Not just the media, our grandparents, our family, they can't forget.

A poll in the *Warsaw Voice* (done by West Berlin Television in July, of 1000 West Germans and 1500 Poles) showed that 58% of Poles think that World War II circumscribes relationship with Germany; 86% think Germans are entirely responsible for the outbreak of that War and 41%, mostly older people are still afraid of the Germans and don't trust them. 53% thought reunification was undesirable at present and only 9% admitted liking Germans. 37% of Germans liked Poles.

Wednesday November 15th
Warsaw

We went to the demonstration outside the Romanian embassy this evening, commemorating the strikes in Brasov two years ago and demanding human rights. A very small turn out for an International day of solidarity: mostly WIP, anarchists, Radical Party, PPS-RD. I had thought, given Ceausescu's call in August for the Warsaw pact to intervene to save Socialism in Poland and prevent a Solidarity government being formed, that there might be more. It was icy cold. We lit candles, listened to some speeches. People were shouting a slogan I hadn't heard before, "Europe without frontiers." Nothing stirred in the embassy.

Thursday November 16th
Warsaw

Janek told us this evening about two Czech miners who turned up in Warsaw today seeking political asylum (they were connected with Charter 77). They had gone to a police station and immediately been arrested. So they asked for Kuron and a director from the Ministry of Labour had gone to sort it out. Later Janek met this director in the ministry. "The man is a former colonel in the Polish army and current party member," Janek explained. "I'm sure he had connections with the Czech secret police. Yet he was incensed saying: 'How could the police be so stupid as to arrest them? Couldn't they see these were political refugees?' His concern was how to get them to Austria. He could help with finance of course but would the Austrians appreciate they needed political asylum?"

The Czech government have now taken their revenge for the Wroclaw conference. Poles are only allowed 24 hours transit visa across Czechoslovakia instead of the usual 48 hours. It's hard to see how long this can all go on, surrounded as they are by a growing sea of democracy.

Friday November 18th
Warsaw

I had a discussion with Piotr O. this evening that finally made me understand why everyone I know is so preoccupied with the German border question. "You have to have a clearly defined state," he said. "If this has no permanency then nothing is possible." I realise that part of my discomfort comes from the fact that at home, especially under Thatcher, the "State" is not something I like very much. But at least it is there, fairly clearly defined, so that its benefits can be protected and excesses challenged. What has happened in Communist Society is that the party, by making itself synonymous with the State, has so intruded into every aspect of the legislature, judiciary, work, education, and people's personal lives that in a sense society is "Stateless." Nor is this the Anarchist vision of a self organised society with "no state." The Party/State is nowhere, because it is everywhere, atomising people's lives. And this in a country where, as Piotr continued, "most of our history has been connected with the question of 'having' or 'not having' a state." So if now Society wants to establish a democratic one, territorial integrity – that is knowing where this state is located and that the boundaries are permanent – becomes crucial, simply in order to begin.

Tuesday November 21st
Gdansk

The thing about Jacek Kuron is that, with his workman's shirt and kindly face he looks so reasonable one feels compelled to believe him. His regular chat shows are masterly television. Tonight he told us that there simply isn't enough money and everyone should contribute to charity, to help those less fortunate. This was after the new-style TV news. It changed this weekend: less comment and more very glossy packaging. "It used to be like listening to your headmaster," Adam G. said, "now it's like going to MacDonalds."

We were having dinner with him, Anja and two West German doctors who had just driven from West Berlin with a car full of medicine for Gdansk Children's hospital. Rainer said he had had to listen to three different radio stations on the morning of the

10th November before he could believe the wall was down. Yes, it was wonderful in some ways, but both the East German opposition and West German Greens had reservations. "There's no chance now of any alternative socialism developing from below. The opposition will just be swallowed up by West German Capital. They can't wait. And none of us in the Alternative are ready – we have no 'concept' of what kind of Europe we want."

I must say I always find the concept of "concepts" slightly worrying. The more total they are the more frightening. I'm not sure ad hoc day to day arrangements and "muddling through" are not in the long run safer and more flexible.

Adam showed us a letter from an East German friend written at the beginning of November. She was writing from her "new home town of Lubeck" having made the decision to leave East Germany in three hours in "a kind of panic," when a friend rang from Budapest, saying she also was leaving. The woman simply got on the train and left, via Hungary and Austria, feeling all her friends were going and there was nothing for which to stay. Now she felt it was the wrong decision, especially when she heard from family. "But not everything is sadness"; she had a nice job in a video cassette shop, where there were interesting people, and a flat with balcony in a nice suburb. . . . The letter reeked of unhappiness. Adam didn't know if she had gone back.

Wednesday November 22nd
Gdansk

There is a hunger strike going on at the Container terminal in Gdynia. It appears that two containers for the reactor at Zarnowiec were being brought in (a Yugoslav boat carrying Czech parts). The boat arrived on Thursday and initially the dockers (all Solidarity) refused to unload it. Then some kind of agreement was reached and the parts were unloaded. At this point the protestors blockaded the road so the special transporters sent from Radom were sent back empty. The containers now sit in the terminal and some twenty hunger strikers sit in the lobby. The director of the port has said he doesn't mind for the moment, although he hopes they will move before a visiting Swedish delegation arrive.

We went up to visit them and Tomas Terlecki, knowing I was

a doctor, asked me to check everyone's ketones, handing me a neatly labelled rack of urine samples and jar of dip sticks. They were all right, although one man looked quite ill. He said he felt fine. He had to continue, he was here "to test if democracy really existed in Poland." He felt that whether nuclear power was truly dangerous or not, people's anxiety and tension about it was a kind of oppression. They were demanding a referendum on the issue of nuclear power and would continue the strike until a decision was made on whether to hold one.

I told Tomas I was amazed they had succeeded in a blockade with seventy people. "Why didn't the police just move you, that's what would happen at home?"

"The government knows if it came down heavily on antinuclear protestors, there would be an outcry. We're not just a few people, there is support all over the country. Twenty cars came from Lublin yesterday, someone brought Red caviar – we couldn't eat it of course. People have said, "if they try to move it – call us – we'll come." All the deputies elected in this region said they were against nuclear power in their campaigns." Even so the press are giving them a bad time – emphasising the youthfulness of the protestors, suggesting they are "hippies and drug addicts," stressing the loss of income to the port, the risk to the containers in subzero temperatures and wasted petrol of the specal transport from Radom.

Kostek Gebert told me the Ministry of Industry vote two weeks ago was 50/50. "This means," he said, "that as there was an equal number of participants on the board, that someone voted both ways. That sums up Poland's state of mind on the issue at the present time."

We took Maria out to lunch. It took some time to persuade her that her favourite dish was not beyond our means at £1.50. Lech Walesa is back in her good books after his speech to the U.S. Congress. "Wonderful, wonderful, I watched it on television and when he raised his arms so . . . and looked down so . . .," she demonstrated lifting both hands in a V, then sighed "It was just like old times. And you know he asked for help for all of Eastern Europe, not just Poland." It was a brilliant speech, whereas before even loyal Solidarity Union members like Leshek Budrewicz were saying "Lech Walesa, he's a very good man, our historical leader, but for today it's enough"; since it was made, I haven't heard a word of criticism.

"What did you think about the wall coming down, Maria?" Another sigh and she lit a Camel cigarette. "My dear, everyday another unimaginable thing happens. I simply cannot predict any more – maybe we will have the third world war." Somehow Maria manages to make such a suggestion sound like a tedious social engagement.

Giedymin's baby Rotweiler is sick with what looks like distemper. It was moving restlessly around the flat, alternately shitting and vomiting, with Giedymin distractedly cleaning up after it and Miscza, his son trying to soothe it. They had already taken it to the vet for intravenous fluid. "He should have been vaccinated but there was none available at the right time," Giedymin said angrily, while making tea. There is something heartrending about an animal in pain: it's incomprehension at its own distress and one's own uselessness in the face of it.

Thursday November 23rd
Sopot

Sopot is deep in snow. We walked on the pier this morning, a sharp white finger in a steel grey sea: some thousand tufted duck bobbing in the water around us, seemingly all asleep with heads tucked under their wngs.

Gosza and Adam J. are back from Holland and planning to go to Moscow. In between times Solidarity have given Gosza money and facilities to organise a natonal conference for Trade Union women, this weekend. She has telexed each region asking them to send someone, saying accommodation and food are provided. Not all the replies have been favourable. One region telexed back saying "if the Union has money to waste, better spend it on single mothers." Quite a few women were coming however, particularly from the smaller towns. Gosza doesn't appear to mind being somewhat out on a limb. Her own thinking about feminism had developed quite gradually over the last few years, through contact with western women, reading and thinking. Now she found she noticed things she hadn't seen before. Like this morning: she had been, as press, to the election of the president of Gdansk. "A woman was standing as candidate and the way she was treated was quite different. For example when she said that, at 35, she was young for the position, everyone laughed; of course it is young for a political post, but they were all joking and nudging each other – and she sensed it. She tried to go on, saying there were some differences between her and the male candidates, and of course they all roared with laughter again. She wanted to talk about her feelings. . . ." Gosza was cleaning fish as she talked and piling the filleted pieces in front of her neatly. "And today the sort of thing that happens everyday, happened again. There weren't enough chairs in the press box, so two male journalists were joking that perhaps the pretty woman – me – would sit on their knees." She grimaced. "They were upset of course that I wasn't flattered. As far as they were concerned it was a compliment."

Although Adam J. is totally supportive, not all her radical friends are. *Acapella* has a "feminist page" but the editorial board turned down an article by Gosza on "rape in marriage." "They said it was 'stupid' and such things don't happen in Poland. If I wanted to publish it I could start my own magazine."

Anja is facing difficulties with work. The job at the children's hospital turns out to be in paediatric radiology and ultrasound and the chief told her there would be no supervision. She would have to train herself. This would require working all day and studying all night, and funding herself to go on courses. Books could not be taken out of the library and anyway Anja only had two hours baby sitting a day. She felt very depressed about it all. It was three and a half years since she had been able to work. "Can't Adam take time off work?" I asked.

"Impossible," she said.

Friday November 24th
Gdansk

Giedymin's dog has died. One small casualty of the current difficulties. Miscza is distraught and Giedymin upset, of course, but he still agreed to come along and translate for an interview with Andrej Gwiazda, whom he likes.

This created some problems. T. and I had arrived early and when Joanna, Gwiazda's wife, heard that Giedymin was coming, said she absolutely could not let him into the flat, as he was a member of the SB (security police). Knowing Giedymin's life for the last eight years, including his phone and passport being removed, this seemed extremely unlikely. Gwiazda was on the phone during her expostulations and took no notice. Giedymin was knocking at the door. T. and I felt acutely embarrassed. Then, fortunately, Gwiazda came off the phone, went to the door, greeted Giedymin warmly and invited him in. Everything seemed to settle down over Vodka and tea.

Gwiazda was a founder of Free Trade Unions in the late seventies and important figure in Solidarity's first legal period. Now under the new government, he was busy organising Free Trade Unions again. He had been totally opposed to the Round table process, feeling that the same degree of political freedom could have been obtained without any compromise. The Round table had just been a means of controlling independent social activity, discrediting the opposition, allowing the Communists to hang onto power, and destroying the Trade union. "I always said Martial law was not because Solidarity demanded power but because it wanted to stay a real trade union. Eight years later, my opinion is confirmed. The Communists are prepared to share power. They can't cope with an independent trade union. That's because the aim of a Communist system is *money* not power. As sole power brokers they were rather inefficient and losing money. They will share power as long as they get profits. That was the real aim of the Round table agreement. And now the party is in dissolution – it's the 'people' who had to pay for their faults at $1000 per head."

He is a thin man with a shock of greying hair and a tired, friendly face. The quiet unemphatic way he spoke contrasted with the certainty of his views. We scarcely needed to ask questions, he had a lot to say.

Solidarity had "betrayed and blinded" society. Registration of the union was recognition of illegitimate authority. Changes in the original statutes were kept secret. It could no longer be considered a Trade union as it was refusing to use the strongest weapon available to protect its members: its ability to strike. It had become Leninist, transmitting the government's message, and creating "a mess in people's minds" so that they no longer knew where their interests lay. "It speaks the same language as the Communists, 'success after sacrifice'. Their activists complain that society is apathetic. I see this as a positive development. People don't want to work. They have ceased to believe in slogans and demand some results from their leaders, not after many years but soon. The only real achievements of Solidarity were free Saturdays and a difference between system and society. Martial law and the repression aimed to destroy these achievements. The new government has succeeded in doing it. Soon," he warned us, "we will have that capitalist dream: a crowd of workers outside the factory gates waiting to be called. Kuron's ideas are not far from this."

In fact some of what Gwiazda was saying was not so different from Leszek Budrewicz's view. Leszek felt that the union, through its constant appeals to people to be patient, was losing moral authority. "People believed when the union was registered, that everything would change rapidly. Of course that's impossible." His solution had been for the government to make the union more of a political partner, "not to treat us as just one, rather inconvenient, element in the situation. To realise that the man in the street identifies the government with the union and that they (the government) can't continue without our support."

Janek's view was that yes, the Round Table was a compromise but only the Communists lost. "A long wave of strikes would have been a disaster for this country. The round table avoided a revolution. By that I mean hangings in the street, firing on demonstrators." He felt that the government could cope with opposition trade unions, "if they attacked the government because it has a bad programme and if they presented a better one linking their material aims to increased productivity. But they only demand more money. This simply preserves the old system. Gwiazda has the same effect as Miodowicz," (leader of the official trade unions, campaigning vigorously against the economic reforms).

But then the question is, is it a trade union's job to present a political programme or it is just to clearly defend one group's interest. Besides which, Gwiazda is not campaigning for more money but less work – an important distinction.

"Just like the Wobblies" said T., "very moral, very logical and very dangerous, because it excludes compromise – it can only result in a clash of interests."

I find myself agreeing with another of Koszek Gebert's articles. He began it with a story:

"Once upon a time there was a country in which one party ruled. The party preached a political doctrine which taught that two and two make seven. Those who said that two and two make four were expelled from work, put in prison and forced to leave the country. However, the time came when the party went through a radical change. The government was taken over by a faction which said that two and two make three. People who claimed that two and two make four were invited for friendly chats and asked: 'Comrade, are you sure you can't see the progress? Would you rather have that dreadful time back when two and two made seven?' "

He went on to argue that you need the uncompromising as it pushes the compromisers to reconsider, at every moment, whether they have got it right and met the needs of as many groups as possible. Moreover if a government, particularly one of national unity, in a new democracy, pushes radical opposition aside because it upsets the "social consensus," the only choice that opposition has is to work against the system as a whole, and threaten the democracy itself.

Monday November 27th
Warsaw

There was a woman begging outside the University this morning. I have seen gypsies beg before here, but not Polish women. This one was old, in headscarf, cheap boots, thick coat and no gloves. She held an empty cigarette tin and sat eyes cast down, saying nothing. It was freezing cold. Quite a few people stopped. Kuron said a few weeks ago that foodstamps canot be issued for the poor after all, because the machinery required to print them is too expensive. The Czechs seem to have crossed the same watershed as the East Germans: continuing to demonstrate in the face of extreme violence and the violence ceasing. The demonstrations have been going on all week in Prague and other cities, each one larger than the last. T. and I argue over the meaning of all this. I feel incredibly excited by this land slide effect of popular pressure: how demonstrations in one country seem to enable those in another; how people seem to gain confidence in themselves, find their way over borders, in defiance of regulations, demonstrate in the street, demand resignations, call strikes and in response, the government makes concession after concession. T. agrees the governments are on the defensive but sees it as Communism showing its ability to transform itself and hang onto power, making only those concessions that are absolutely necessary. "All Krenz had to do was open the borders and now he is taken seriously by the West. Look at this long interview in the paper." He pointed to the Saturday's *Financial Times* with half a page given over to the East German leader, looking very much a Western politician in his photograph. "And Dubcek still talks of 'Socialism with a human face'! It doesn't have one."

Mrs Thatcher apparently thinks the pace of reform is a little too fast in Eastern Europe. "In some senses it is a little fast for *us*," Janek commented . . . "It means we are no longer first in line."

Tuesday November 28th
Warsaw

We spent this afternoon with the president of the Co-ordinative Council of the Polish National Movement. Mr Tejkowski claims "10,000 organised members" and has an ideology that would be terrifying were it not for the fact that he appears to be unable to buy a new shirt. His current one is too small and lacks some buttons so that it gapes to reveal hairy torso, ill concealed by a smartly knotted tie. He had been "delighted" to talk to us when we rang and kissed my hand gravely when we arrived, ushering us into a tiny bedsit. The floorspace was consumed by a large bed, covered with piles of cyclostiled literature and a table around which two colleagues were already seated: a smart looking woman in a red dress and a tall thin man in a worn three-piece suit. His cuffs were frayed and he had the hands of a manual worker, with blackened nails. A third man arrived late, thickset, in a pullover, clutching bundles of Poland's main university weekly, of which he was the editor. It contained an interview with Mr Tejkowski. They had provided cake for us but not for themselves. "Great parties start small and poor," the editor joked, urging us to eat. The walls of the room were covered by two large maps: one of 11th century Poland showing ethnic groups, the other showing the geographical areas of Poland and Lithuania. Crowned eagles of wood, plaster and metal hung from strategic points and a portrait of Dmowski stared down at me from crowded bookshelves.

Since the change of government the national idea had "surfaced with vigour," Mr Tejkowski explained. Not that he had any liking for Solidarity, seeing it as determined to preserve the monopolistic structure of power. As far as he was concerned, the Round Table process simply transferred power from the Communists to Solidarity, "New forms, the same principles." "All political parties are still illegal under the existing regulations. Mazowiecki doesn't represent the national interest. He is paying the Communist debt by selling off Poland's assets to the Germans." Mr Tejkowski's manner was quiet and measured. On ideological issues he deferred, with a bow of the head, to the thin man in the three-piece suit who ponderously explained the problem of "national minorities." "We have doubts as to whether the intentions of some people are sincere. It would be correct to think that in this context national interest is endangered by foreign factors who use these minorities as a tool against us: Kohl with the Silesians or the Jews at Auschwitz for example." The editor interrupted emotionally, "The problem is our economic situation, they can play with us as they like. Look!" He leapt up to the map. "Kohl will invest German money in Polish enterprises only in what was previously 'German' Poland." He banged the map with his hand, drawing a line down through what was once West Prussia. "What is THAT do you think?" "And Auschwitz," I asked tentatively, "what's the solution there?" The editor exploded, first in Polish then translating himself into English. "Only Poland! The one STUPID example in the whole fucking world . . . excuse my language . . . where the world is coming now and trying to take something from us. What the Jews are doing now in Auschwitz is one of the most horrible anti-Polish aggressions I have ever seen! Look what we have prepared for them! The great amount of monuments, the possibilities for praying, total facilities connected with their memories, it's absolutely enough! It's too much! Look at Poznan, streets reconstructed strictly as in Prussian times. I am absolutely against the stupid game of always worrying what others think of us!"

Drops of spit had settled on my tape recorder. I felt a little sick. No one seemed to be put out by the outburst. Mr Tejkowski wished to explain more about nationalism: of course the rights of minorities would always be protected, but they were against the Liberalism which put individual rights higher than those of the community. The national community was the supreme good and there was a right and duty to achieve what was good for it, by their own strength but not at the cost of other nations, of course. "The question is who should govern the Polish nation? Stalin's people, many of whom are Jews, or honest patriots?"

"National unity is based on a socialist tradition but doesn't stress the class struggle, preferring to see classes as having complementary interests. It is the national interest that is the real criterion for distinguishing Left and Right." He was all for a market economy with no limit on profits and did not see unemployment as a problem: "Public works can be introduced to deal with this, canal and road building for example." As for women, "It is in the nature of things that woman's role is determined by her maternal role. If she has a baby she should not be allowed to work until the child is six." "A man could take this role" he conceded generously in deference to my challenging this comment, but one parent must stay at home, "the family is the centre of the nation."

I retreated to the tiny bathroom where clean washing was neatly piled in a plastic bowl next to metal weights on the floor. Mr Tejkowski is a muscular, well preserved man. When I came out, another elderly man in worn three-piece had arrived. He also kissed my hand. A meeting of the Council was about to begin so we made our farewells. "Any help we can give you, anything we can do for you at all, don't hesitate to let us know," said Mr Tejkowski. "The national idea has been incriminated under the Communists, now it is reawakening and our job is to organise."

Outside it was freezing. The icy pavement penetrating through the soles of my boots so that it was hard to stand still. I found myself suddenly hypersensitive to certain kinds of graffiti: swastikas, a jewish star hanging from a gallows. I felt depressed by the atmosphere of slightly squalid poverty and the effort made on our behalf, and uneasy at the potential force of "the national idea." Too easy to dismiss them as marginal. Kostek said something very similar to Krzysztof regarding youth. "Pacifists and green groups are too permissive, young people want a pre-packed ideology with simple answers like "Poland is not run by Poles but Jews and Russians." Since he wrote his article on the controversy over Auschwitz, he had had a stream of hate mail. The letters were all signed and from all ages and classes, saying the usual: "You guys run the world," "It's high time all the Yids left." His son has been ganged up on, at school, Poland is "benignly antisemitic," he feels. What does it take to make it less benign?

Wednesday November 29th
Warsaw

Had to meet Elzbieta off the early morning train. As the streets are like skating rinks at the moment, I went to the taxi rank nearby. There were three quite smartly dressed young men standing there, stamping their feet in the snow. They were all dark skinned and smiled at me politely as I joined the queue. Two taxis immediately pulled up. The three men stepped forward to the first and I to the second. As I was getting in, I saw the first taxi pull off without waiting for the boys to reach it. I stepped back offering mine and it pulled away as well. A third came up and the men indicated to me to get in, which I did, guiltily feeling that I was somehow colluding in something unpleasant.

Elzbieta was her usual caustic self staring gloomily at the Marriott as we drove by. "They are planning a Christmas ball there at $1000 a head and the tickets are sold out already. There are rumours about that place, all over Poland."

Back at the flat we had to have a cold breakfast in semidarkness as all the electricity blew last night. Janėk patiently tried to guide us through mending Polish fuses over the phone this morning, but the problem appears to run deeper. "I see you are not shopping in Polish shops," Elzbieta remarked, eyeing the French Brie.

"We had a party," I said feeling guilty. Elzbieta feels I do not experience Polish reality to a sufficient degree and that I should live on a Polish income and always shop and queue in Polish shops. She's right in one sense of course, "but I would never get my research done in the allotted time!" I moan.

"Exactly!" she responded, "that's the reality." We talked about East Germany. Apparently Poles are now having to show identity cards in shops, some of which have signs saying "no Poles." She felt depressed by this and the possiblity of an anti-german backlash.

Elzbieta wanted to see the World Press Photo 89 exhibition, donated at vast expense by the Dutch government, so we went over to the museum by the Hotel Victoria. It was very crowded. What struck me was how every single prize winning news photo was of violence or disaster: IRA/loyalist killings, falling aeroplanes, flood, famine, chemical warfare. The single nonviolent image in the whole News section was of Gdansk shipyard workers on strike.

Is it just that positive events aren't newsworthy or photographic? Perhaps this year will be different.

I am feeling a little battered over the head by the news at the moment. If you glance away for a moment, you have missed another world shattering event. The Baltics have been given economic autonomy, 200,000 people are demonstrating in Leipzig, and now the banners say "Germany, one Nation." Kohl has said German unity is a long term goal. The Czechs have had a successful general strike, their politbureau has resigned, their opposition umbrella group, Civic Forum is negotiating with the new prime minister Adamec, and the parliament have voted for free elections and a multiparty system. Meanwhile Lech Walesa was on Sky television, sitting with Ron Todd and Norman Willis, all in suits and looking rather similar, saying the Polish economy is like an old car that needs new parts to make it go again. "Old car!" scoffed Sigismund, "it's not just repairs! we need an entirely new model!"

T. has been getting calls from home all day. Apparently "The Serbs are coming." This did not feature on Sky news. Probably the complexity of Yugoslav politics is too much to encompass in its rather slick one liners. The Serbs decided they wanted to discuss the "problems" in Kosovo (where Albanians live under Martial law, imposed by Serbia) directly with the Slovene people who have "not understood just how inhuman the Albanians are and keep protesting about human rights." So Serbians planned a mass demonstration in Slovenia on December 1st (the date of the founding of the old, Serbian dominated Yugoslav kingdom). Slovenia has reacted by declaring a state of emergency to protect its population and the alternative organisations have declared three days culture silence – a move not taken since Nazi occupation.

Thursday November 30th
Gdansk

"The Serbs are not coming." They have frozen relations with Slovenia instead. And while the rest of Europe is in process of rejecting Communism, the Slovenian Communist government has never been so popular. Many people are rejoining the Party. "Of course," said T. resignedly, "it is a forced choice between Slovene liberal Communism and Serbian orthodox Communism. A national threat pushes all other problems aside." Nothing like an external enemy for creating unity at home.

We went up to the port in Gdynia again to see how the hunger strikers were. Most of them have moved into town and only a small picket continues at the port. The demonstrators looked younger than ever. I did a quick poll: one plump blond school girl from the "Federation of Fighting Youth"(FMW), one quiet young man from "Wole bye" (I want to be: an unstructured youth movement, centred around a popular magazine), two from "Twe Twa," two "independent," unaffiliated young men, a boy with a half shaved head from "Anarchist Intercity" and one pet rat, very sleepy. They told us the hungerstrike, though not the picket, would end that night but restart on Monday if the promise of a referendum was not forthcoming. And would we join the demonstration that evening in Gdansk?

Gosza was feeling very pleased with the success of the Solidarity Trade Union Women's conference. "About thirty women came from different regions. At the beginning two women said they had only come to express their concern at Solidarity being split into two halves but by midday they said they were convinced we did need a women's 'commission'. What convinced them apparently were data about membership. The rank and file membership is 40% women. yet it's less than 5% of the governing body. "Though actually we don't have accurate data, the first thing we have decided to do is to collect it."

She read out the other decisions that they had made from a cyclostiled sheet, commenting as she went:

– To develop women's consciousness. "Women simply accept their lower positions in the workplace and the fact that they don't get directorships. And although there is good legislation for maternity leave it's often hard for younger women to get jobs because of the risk of pregnancy, and it will get harder."

– To create a better social infrastructure: with creches and "intervention centres." "It was their idea. If a husband is drinking up the family wages they plan to have a group of women who can assist the wife in getting money from him, to support the children and herself."

– To live and work in a healthy environment. "The representative from Czestochowa included a demand that women in the cotton mills should get a pension after thirty years, regardless of age, because of the tropical conditions in which they work. And they also made a unanimous statement against nuclear power."

– To have Saturdays free.

And finally, "women should be guaranteed representation in the decision making bodies, that reflects real membership."

The women were going to present the postulates in each region and encourage others to join the local "commission." "We have suggested there should be someone paid and we want permanent representatives at the executive level." For the time being this would be Gosza and another friend.

Gosza felt a little surprised at how much the meeting had achieved. "It is really demanding a lot! This isn't the West. It may even be seen as shocking. A revolution is taking place. "Apparently only a few women teachers came from Gdansk region. "Some nurses wanted to come and the rumour is that Borusewicz discouraged them – but that's *only* gossip," Gosza smiled.

Adam J. came back from the prison where he had been writing about the strike. We had seen the men on the roof and the banners when we came in this morning on the train. This strike started on the 18th November apparently, when prisoners heard that an amnesty being discussed in Parliament would not cover all categories of prisoners. The prisoners had disarmed a guard, taken the keys and taken over a wing. Cells were unlocked but any prisoners causing trouble were relocked in their cells by the prisoners own strike committee. "The authorities are taking a very softly, softly approach because we have had some horrible prison riots, with lives lost," Adam said.

Then we all piled into a taxi to get to the old town in time for the anti-Zarnowiec demonstration. This time it was not just a small bunch of radicals, but a large crowd of people of all ages gathered around the old town hall steps, now draped with banners. In the flickering candle light the faces looked pale, serious, and timeless.

On the train going home we met a priest who argued that Poland had to have nuclear energy because of the pollution and radioactivity of coal. This is a common argument in this country, but ignores the fact that there is no possibility or intention of closing down any existing coal fired powerplants at the present time. Yet while money is poured into the nuclear programe it is not available to modernise the existing plants or build dust extractors.

Janek, who is not particularly concerned about the safety aspects, sees nuclear energy as an expensive fantasy of the previous government that is completely beyond Poland's means and that makes no economic sense. Kostek G. hopes the IMF will have the sense to ban it.

Our priest was a very pleasant man, bespectacled, white haired, with an English public schoolmaster manner, he murmured, mildly, that after all he knew very little about it. He had been sitting in the corner of our compartment and reading a *Young Poland* newspaper and we had got into one of those long conversations that one only seems to have with complete strangers on train journeys.

He had Polish parents who had emigrated in the War and he himself had only came back a month ago. Now he had a parish of 33,000 in the Praga (a district in Warsaw) and felt quite depressed by people's poverty and resignation. "The system has destroyed any enthusiasm for work. We need massive amounts of aid, not just the odd $100 million here and there. That will just about replace Warsaw's telephone exchange and can you imagine business men functioning with the current one. If the West would spend the bllions it spends on armaments on aid to Eastern Europe and the USSR, it would have far more security and a huge new market."

But his main preoccupation was banks – or rather the lack of any Western style ones in Poland. "Poles keep three to twenty billion dollars in their mattresses, that's a guess. Each of those one million people who work abroad every year bring home about $2000, that's ten billion and because we have no banks in which people can invest we are losing one billion dollars interest a year." He rattled off the figures in a very unpriestly way, he had obviously been giving the matter some thought.

"My idea is that the church should run a bank. Think of it . . . we have plenty of rooms, shopkeepers get their change from us anyway on Mondays, after Sunday collection. We're present in every village, so it would be ideal for farmers and we are moral, legal and creditworthy. The Church and a western bank in partnership would have people's confidence. I've presented the idea to my boss, he was a little taken aback."

"Your boss?"

"Cardinal Glemp, he's a slow, reserved sort of man. Very good.

'But we're losing one million dollars a day in interest', I said to him, 'delay costs money.' Of course Solidarity wants its own bank . . .".

The train was pulling in. He shook our hands vigorously and gave us his card. I somehow felt he was in the wrong profession; perhaps not – priest and backmanager may be an ideal combination in this country.

Saturday December 2nd
Warsaw

Not all nationalists live in impoverished bedsits. There is a civilised face: The Christian National Union was formed two months ago. It already has a membership of 10,000, and has as its president Mr Chrzanowski, legal adviser to Solidarity in 1980, author of the Trade union's original statutes and adviser to Glemp. Prominent Solidarity leaders like Jan Rulewski are members as are Ludwik Dorn and Antonin Macierewicz, former members of KOR.

Macierewicz explained to us this morning, that while KOR had not been ideological, and its main concern had been to restructure society outside state structures, through independent social organisations like free trade unions, there had always been two wings. "The Left: Kuron, Geremek etc. treated these institutions instrumentally, as an element of pressure on the authorities, with whom they later wanted an alliance. They always wanted that alliance. And when I read in the papers today that Adam Michnik thinks party liberals like Rakowski should join the pragmaticians in Solidarity like himself, I see the tactic is still there. Our concern on the right was to restructure the Polish state as a Democratic National State."

In fact, for both Macierewicz and Dorn, whom we saw last night, the National idea is not a belief or idea to be discussed or promoted. It is a 'given'. Poland is 98% Polish, and Catholic, so it is "one nation." "A common national identity means common convictions, resulting from historical experiences that unite the nation," said Macierewicz. "One obvious one is that any German-Russian agreement is murderous. The other is Catholicism."

For Dorn the Catholic faith provides "the social framework and source of values" for Polish people. The Christian National Party, of which he is vice chair, would simply give these political expression. He summarised the values for us as "Solidarity before conflict," "the principle of common good," and "helpfulness" which all sounded nice, but vague, and in practice seems to mean the private individual should do as much as possible for himself and others and if it's not enough in the case of charity, or too much in the case of ecological damage, the state should intervene. Dorn would also enshrine the role of the church and Catholicism in the new constitution to emphasise the part it has played in creating the nation. He didn't see this as legalistic, simply stating an established fact, though it would have legal consequences. Abortion for example would be unconstitutional. "The state should provide the conditions for citizens to lead a moral and virtuous life."

Macierewicz was more moderate. Traditional and Christian morality should be taught in schools, particularly in subjects such as "preparation for family life." There was no such thing as neutral teaching in such an area and trying to teach a diversity of views simply "destroyed social ties as effectively as Communism has done."

No, this was not imposing an ideology in the same way as the Communists had tried to impose Socialism. That was the imposition of ideas by a minority, and therefore "Bolshevism," while Catholicism expressed the feeling of the majority; and their right to influence education according to tradition. As for minorities, "they should, as in every democratic country, respect the majority decision." Their right to autonomy would be respected of course. "In any case," Dorn explained, "I do not stress national homogeneity, as now it is a fact and for a mainly homogeneous nation, minorities are useful. They make social and cultural life much more interesting. It was quite different before the War when minorities imposed a danger to social equilibrium."

"And there is no strong antisemitism in Poland," he assured us. "The debate over Auschwitz was due mainly to the activities of American Jews. There was a genuine religious difference between the Jews and Catholics, but this was politicised by American East Coast Jews, to exert pressure on the Catholic Church." Dorn explained that he was of "half Jewish origin" himself. He didn't see it as a conspiracy. "But they are a group that can exert influence through the *New York Times* and *Washington Post.* It's not dangerous, it's normal for any ethnic group. I wish the American Polish minority were as effective. And you should understand," he added, "that it is part of an internal Polish quarrel. Some important persons and groups in the opposition are of Jewish origin and they label their opponents as antisemitic. Kostek Gebert? He is not a Pole, he said so himself, and he is not a serious person."

Ludwik Dorn's apartment could not have been more different from Tejkowski's. Built for the apparatchiki and stahanovci, it was inhabited by a Jewish public prosecutor until he left in 1968. Dorn and his family had moved there in 1970. We had sat in a white painted room with polished floor and antique furniture. A beautiful rug decorated one wall, a woodcut and small painting the other. Dorn, in his hand knitted sweater and hand knitted socks, had explained that the chauvinistic excesses of nationalism could be limited, firstly by strong cultural identity. "Because this creates self confidence. If you feel strong you have no reason to be aggressive." And second, "by the Catholic religion, which is universal and limits aggressive feelings for other nations." I still felt uneasy.

For one thing there are so many inconsistencies. Dorn feels that each nation has the right to self determination but, when considering German unification, Polish political and national interests should be considered. " 'Europe without frontiers' is a German smokescreen for unification." Macierewicz insists that teachers should have the "freedom" to teach as they wish but that certain books (on sex education for example) should be withdrawn. That individual rights should be respected but that "equal rights" for a woman "humiliates and destroys her because she has to work twice as hard." The idea that he might do the housework himself did not seem to have crossed his mind. He argued that the minority should respect the majority but that if his view on the criminality of abortions were a minority opinion then the majority would have to be challenged, because his view conformed with "natural law."

And paradoxically – while both see their opinions as representing a Catholic, national social consensus, they strongly objected to the "family" dominated OKP claiming to represent a social consensus themselves. They view this "leftist" "elite" as obstructing the development of real political pluralism in order to retain their "monopoly of power." "First there was one 'subject', now there are two," said Dorn. "They use the mystical unity of the Solidarity movement to create a monopolistic patronage club, because they don't want to be a part, they want to represent the whole."

"The 'family' are too weak to make a party," was Macierewicz's comment. "If they did there would turn out to be only five and they couldn't act in the name of the nation." He felt, sounding like Gwiazda, that "without the Round table, Jaruzelski would have been forced to go, just like Honecker." The fuse for change in Eastern Europe was Gorbachev not Poland.

Still, he supported Mazowiecki, as did Dorn. "A progressive liberal Catholic is better than Mr Kuron," and it was an important counterbalance to the monopolistic tendencies of the OKP. Though Dorn seemed unperturbed at the prospect of presidential rule, if Mazowiecki failed.

My other problem is that I am still groping for the value in the concept of "Nation." This "thing" which is the "natural environment" for the individual; for which, according to St Thomas Aquinas (quoted with almost religious fervour by Dorn) one has "more responsibility than the rest of humanity"; and to which one has a "certain moral bond" and "obligation." I can understand that, because of common language, culture, belief or simply out of the affection that comes with neighbourliness and familiarity, one might feel closer to certain individuals than others, more at home in one landscape than another. But I have never understood why those feelings should imbue their objects with MORE intrinsic value than that of another person of another culture or another landscape, equally loved by someone else. Why should something be morally superior just because it is 'familiar'?

Monday December 4th

Krakow, a.m.

Jan Maria Rokita has gained the weight that so often seems to accompany an entry into parliamentary politics but not yet the courtesy.

I met him yesterday at the cafe where Bogdan and his friends meet on Sunday afternoons, and, anxious to hear his side of the election expenses/corruption story, made an appointment for today, making it clear that I was staying an extra day on his account. Today, without phoning me or his staff, he failed to turn up.

Never mind, it gives me time to sit with the money changers in the Alvorado cafe. It's a small place with marble floor, cane chairs, chrome counter and good coffee. You can look out onto the beautiful market square, the towers of St Mary's just visible above the arcaded market building mist dissolving in the sunlight.

The money changers all wear leather or padded jackets. Mostly their hair is a little long. There is only one woman, sharp looking. They count notes from bulging paper packets, finger their pocket calculators and shout the days rate from table to table. Perhaps this is the beginning of a stock exchange. The bank is only across the road.

Yesterday I had an argument with the editor of *Tygodnik Powszechny* (a Catholic weekly) about Social Democracy. He was quite optimistic about the current Polish situation, but felt the new government was too reluctant to let go of a Welfare state. "I know in Britain you're all enamoured with it, but free education and health care simply don't work." He recounted as proof the horrifying story of a kindergarten in Sweden where the teacher had made children celebrate Lenin's birthday and spy on each others capital expenditure. I said I was sad to hear such useful institutions as the NHS dismissed on the basis of one foolish kindergarten teacher, and did he really want a system where how healthy and how educated you were depended on how much money you possessed. "Private charity," he replied, "this is the answer."

Even Piotr O. has shifted his ground since I've been here. Sweden is impossible, without Swedish wealth and to produce it, Poland needs "liberalism." There is the almost universal insistence that Poland has to go through some version of mid-19th century industrial expansion with all its attendant evils. "Social justice kills the market. You have to have a market first with all its negative consequences and then regulate it." The trouble with this for me is that the costs, in terms of human suffering and ecological damage, in an unregulated twentieth century market, may be beyond repair at a later date.

Warsaw, p.m.

I left the Alvorado and went round to the military studies centre of the university, now being occupied by the Krakow student boycott committee. At its annual conference a few weeks ago NZS declared the boycott over, having achieved some reform and the right to negotiate with a parliamentary commission on the subject. Krakow NZS and some other universities formally seceded over the autonomy issue and the Independent Student Boycott Committee, unhappy with the result of the negotiations so far, is trying to continue its campaign.

A thin, rather beautiful, young man with long blond hair and green eyes, pulled a wooden bar out of the swing doors and insisted on giving me a guided tour of every classroom: showing me with disgust the wall posters of Warsaw pact organisation, how to dismantle a rifle, how to put it together again. There was an enormous ugly and very detailed plaster relief of exactly what happens if a nuclear bomb falls complete with burning buildings and mutilated bodies. "What happens if one falls here! or here!" my guide said pointing to nicely organised first aid stations and shelters on the fringes of the blast area . . . Someone had pinned a notice saying "Zarnowiec" at ground zero. "And look at all this," he pointed to overhead projectors, video recorders, and TV screens. "You won't find this equipment in other classrooms. The university has no money. We want the army out of education, that's all!"

The occupation had not had much effect so far. In other universities, students were drifting back. So Krakow were going to occupy the Ministry of Education the next day, in Warsaw.

Went round to see Deborah this evening, just back from covering the Mazowiecki trip to Russia for Associated Press.

"People kept asking me who the Poles were and was Mazowiecki really the Prime Minister."

"Why?"

"Because they all wear short coats and these funny little hats. Minister Hall just had an old hand knitted sweater over his suit. Russians expect their politicians to wear big thick coats and fur hats. And you know when they went to the tomb of the unknown soldier . . .," she imitated the soldiers goosestepping, "I was standing right opposite Mazowiecki – so I saw the expression on his face as this 'parade' went by – complete bewilderment." It's impossible not to feel bewildered oneself in this upside down world where former political prisoners and underground conspirators are now visiting heads of state. My friend Maria in Krakow says she has to keep pinching herself to make sure she's not dreaming.

Tuesday December 5th
Warsaw

It was easy to spot the Krakow students as they stuck out somewhat, sitting with their rucksacks in the corner of the lobby of the Ministry of Education. The lobby was the kind that is largely imposing staircase and not much else, so we progressed up it, without hindrance, and straight into the anteroom of Minister Samsonowicz's office. The secretary looked a little startled, but politely offered the students seats beside the potted plants while she went to see if the Minister was free. "He can see you in an hour," she came out to tell us, "would you mind waiting?" She showed us into a long thin conference room with its statutory eagle on the wall, and high backed chairs. Marcin Maron immediately examined the window for "banner hanging" possibilities, while someone else checked the end door. "What are you going to do?" I asked, still a little stunned at the friendly reception so far. "Oh, negotiate and then we'll see," Marcin said airily.

At 2 p.m the Minister came in, a small man with neatly cut hair in a light brown tweed jacket and woollen vest, he was apologetic. He had not known about the visit so had not planned for it. Would the students like to talk briefly now, or wait until 3 p.m. and talk longer? By now everyone looked completely at home. A black flag had appeared from somewhere. Malinowski's "The Myth of Freedom" from the kiosk downstairs was on the table along with a mass of leaflets, half eaten packed lunches and bottles of orangeade. "Oh 3 p.m. is fine," they replied happily. The Minister left. "The police threw us out of the Ministry of Justice after a few hours last year, but that was last year," Marcin told me.

At 3 p.m. the Minister came back with a colleague, and the discussion began. It went on at length and everyone got quite heated. But after two hours talking they suddenly reached an agreement.

The Minister agreed to the students' right to continue their action and boycott (with the understanding that he was not responsible for the effect on their studies). He could not agree to suspending military classes while negotiations continued. However the Student Boycott Committee should have their own representative on the parliamentary commission. It took 30 minutes for four copies to be typed out and signed by all. Minister Samsonowicz seemed very cheerful, perhaps at the thought that no one was going to hang banners from his conference room windows. "These are extremists," he told me, pulling on his raincoat, his secretary had already left. "But they need representation on the commission. Personally I think the army is a good professional and intellectual preparation for students, but we do have a problem with indoctrination."

Marcin was reasonably happy. "A compromise, last year it would have been impossible, next year it might be again." Marcin is an anarchist from Krakow WIP. He is certain that this is the time when extra parliamentary groups should be most active, because the government is anxious not to appear repressive and has to respond. It's certainly true that these groups, small and 'marginal' as they are, occupy a democratic space that doesn't exist for much larger pressure groups at home. They have an accessibility to government and a self confidence in their right to be heard that we too often seem to lack. While the government, its ministers included, still appears to be sensitive enough to listen. This might be because it is image conscious or perhaps, as Janek suggested some time ago, their experience in the opposition genuinely creates a greater sensibility to these movements and their concerns.

On my way home I called in on Jacek Szymanderski. A sociologist, one time adviser to WIP, now a deputy and chief of the board of Rural Solidarity.

His view was that even though such groups were marginal at the moment, they were essential. "It is only through them that a new culture can be created. They have to start an opposition towards us. Not political – we have the full spectrum – but something more deep. We are the old men, still thinking in a narrow minded petit bourgeois nineteenth century way: nation, state, government. They have to criticise us for being obsolete, create a cultural opposition, an ecological culture perhaps. What does it mean 'border' for Chernobyl? It is only through such groups that you can do away with nationalism. They have to think European. Not Eurpean policy – just European."

However he personally was still very preoccupied with current national problems. Rural Solidarity is in the process of becoming a political party. He estimated that about 30% of the village population supported them. Rural Solidarity trade union had half a million farms as fee paying members which meant an actual membership of 2 million. They needed a party because there were problems that couldn't be solved by a trade union. He didn't see the other two peasant parties: the newly named, formerly procommunist party, or the recreated prewar, old peasants' party as a real threat. The former had no real support outside parliament, and the latter was very right wing.

And if anyone was going to be squeezed in the current economic crisis, he argued, it should not be the peasants. "All political crises have been precipitated by lack of food. You can argue that if there is social unrest in the cities it will sweep away the government. But if the peasants stop production and food prices rise this will also sweep away the government."

Moreover peasants were 40% of the population and if there was going to be massive unemployment and continued housing shortages in the cities, it might be a good idea to keep people housed and productive in the country. In fact Jacek saw "the peasant" as Poland's solution. "Why? because *his* real interest is to *invest*, to invest and accumulate, invest and accumulate. His standard of living is absolutely secondary. Given the choice between a TV set and a work tool he will choose the tool each time. The government is very suspicious of us, as they see us dividing this 'general support' – but 'general support' is a myth."

Jacek sees himself as a "leftist" but not an "elitist." The "elite," mainly from KOR, had through their "intelligence, talent, capacity and wits" contributed to the current situation but now they wanted to hold on to their position as an intellectual and social elite. "They are all for equality as long as it does not include them. They are absolutely against our caucus (the Solidarity Parliamentary club OKP) being divided on political lines. They want it done on themes: economy, military culture – this is not politics! And it's because they are absolutely aware that if it comes to political division, they will be compelled to create their own party and they wll be very weak. That's why they voice so strongly this idea of 'national unity.' "

I had to go and Jacek had a meeting but he didn't want me to leave until he had told me about "the problem with Germany." "*Hate* is the proper word. This feeling against Poland . . . of course it may be whipped up by the Communists but why did it catch on? This is like Antisemitism in 1933–34 in Germany. Police stop people in the street to do a public search. You in the West should not be mute about such things. If it were to break out openly into a pogrom, that would be the end of 'perestroika'. You have to understand they have had sixty years totalitarianism. 1933 was the end of democracy in that part of Germany. They have *no* political structure. We at least had some from '75, '80, enough to create some authority. Czechoslovakia has an old opposition, an independent social elite. You need one to control the political situation. They have nothing. They just started a revolution. I think they are very frustrated, so they are very radical and it creates a quite new kind of nationalism. It is also a reaction for a lost war. Not against the Soviet Union, who were the legitimate winners, but against us, the Poles, who didn't win with our own muscles. It is mysticism but . . . And our feeling is, of course, that in some sense they were winners, and Communism kept a muzzle on them. I always said that all these feelings were frozen in 1945. So after the collapse of Communism, everything is melting – it is 1945." Jacek saw me to the door, emphasising again as we stood in the hall. "Don't underestimate the problem. It's absolutely serious. It's not just a problem between Poles and Germans. It is about this nationalist way of thinking. It is *the* most serious problem of Perestroika."

Wednesday December 6th
Warsaw

I succeeded in thoroughly irritating Adam Michnik this morning by putting to him the accusations of the "left" and the "right" that the current parliament was an "alliance between the red and the pink," and that parts of the OKP were "elitist" and determined to hang on to their monopoly of power.

"Idiotic! In every country you have people with crazy ideas." He made a twisting gesture with his hand by his head, "unfortunately Poland is not free of them. Everyone now has far more possibility to organise than before the Round table." We were not having the discussion in an atmosphere conducive to patience. We were sitting in his tiny room at *Gazeta*, with its window on to the chaos in the outer office. Our chairs crammed between three desks and a table. Adam had chosen the time, but he was combining it with reading three newspapers.

"The government has been confirmed by the majority of society," he continued. "It was not smply an anticommunist vote. If they had wanted other candidates or parties like Moczulski, they would have voted for them. There was a 'national consensus' at the moment, bearing no resemblance to the 'consensus' described by Macierewicz.

Gazeta published an opinion poll yesterday showing that 'us' is now 'Government, Sejm, Senate, Church, Solidarity,' while 'them' is 'PZPR, ZSL, SD OPZZ, police and army.' (TV is somewhere in the middle). At the beginning of the year 'us' was just Church and Solidarity.)" So this would appear to bear Adam out. And yes, "the consensus was 'healthy' and 'necessary' in a country 'building democracy'. The longer it exists, the longer chance we have to move into democracy without civil war . . . In my view the prewar structure of multiparties wll not be rebuilt in Poland now. The parties that are going to occupy the political scene will be those founded and grown from the new reality . . . A new form will emerge from all the structures that are organically constructed in the body of Polish Society – Solidarity is such a movement." The problem was that while the "social base" for such a movement existed it had not yet apparently "gained an awareness of its power." He saw the citizens committees as the basis of this new "movement" – not party – "It's a dirty word in Poland and we are trying to avoid the social trauma connected with the word". If people in the committees didn't like the idea, they could leave and form their own parties. No one prevented them.

It all sounded very reasonable. The problem for me is that it would seem a great deal easier to get political support for an idea that already has a power base, in established structures like the trade union and local citizens' committees and in a friendly press, than for one that must start from scratch. Just as the only parliamentary candidates freely elected were those endorsed by Lech Walesa. Of course, one could argue that the Solidarity movement *earned* that power base through its own courageous struggle in far harder times. But isn't the real test of a group's commitment to democracy its ability, once in power, to share those resources that give access to power: like funds and media space.

"Anyone who wants, can found a newspaper," said Adam, but he did not have to finance his own. While a Green Federation friend told me, he would love to start one, but simply didn't have the means.

"Why was *Gazeta Wyborcza*'s column for differing opinions abandoned?" I asked.

"It stopped being interesting. How often can one read about Soviet tanks being based in Poland, about Jewish masons and economists being responsible for all our problems, or that our paper is antichristian, and anti church? Actually I think we should reintroduce it, but I don't have a clear editorial idea."

"And what about Social movements. Do they contribute to democracy?"

"They have some positive tendencies, but they can be very destabilising." At this point we were interrupted by Helena and a small entourage carrying documents relating to the breakdown of some relationship with the Italians. A lot of people in the office were talking at once. Adam, leapt to his feet, waving his arms, shouting "Bitch." However he knew someone, who knew someone, and it would all be sorted out.

We offered to go, but Adam wanted to finish his point about social movements. "For example, this mess about the Lenin monument was very negative. (The statue of Lenin in Nowa Huta, Krakow had been set on fire by a crowd of demonstrators on the day before Mazowiecki's visit to the Soviet Union. Debby had told us that the Soviet Ambassador was *very* upset. The protests were still rumbling on.)

"Is that just because it was a violent protest?" I asked.

"No, if the government is legal you must act legally," Adam insisted. "If it is regarded as illegal by society, then all kinds of protests are justifiable. You can not demonstrate against Pinochet and Allende in Chile in the same way. We have a government based on social agreement and there are legal ways available."

"But nonviolent civil disobedience is sometimes the only way a minority can express its view even in a democratic society."

"And what are the limits of the anarchisation of society?" He jabbed his finger at me. "Supposing you want an abortion; that is your legal right, and you come to the hospital and it is occupied by women from the Catholic Antiabortion movement? What then? Hm? What will you do? What are the limits of protest?" He nodded triumphantly and after kissing my hand and smiling charmingly, rushed off to deal with the Italians, so I had no chance to reply that my limits were the use of violence. That, in my experience, when minorities had strongly held views that were outside the social consensus, expressed in a country's legal statutes, they didn't usually choose between "action" and "restraint" but between "nonviolent" and "violent" action. I would rather those against abortion chose nonviolent occupation than hate mail and death treats; and I would prefer fascists to sit down in the street to burning down synagogues. The former actions offer the possibility of dialogue, the latter maim and destroy, that is what counts.

Nonviolent action still seems to be toppling heads of State. Today is Wednesday: it must be East Germany – Krenz has resigned first as party leader, now as head of state. Too many booing crowds. Honecker is under house arrest for corruption and the Czechs are threatening another general strike if more suitable candidates are not proposed for the new government. Unlike the Poles they are not going to accept a Communist Minister of Interior or Defence. It's extraordinary how the time frame for change speeds up in each country.

Thursday December 7th
Warsaw

I had to spend this afternoon in the Police station again as my purse was stolen in the grocers. They recognised me and were as friendly as before. I am beginning to quite like the ordinary Polish police. There is one on the roundabout outside the Hotel Forum who has stopped me three times, just to check my vehicle documents and propose marriage. This time the process took longer than last because my officer, young and moustached, took time off to talk to his wife on the telephone. She had had a baby yesterday and as he and her father were drinking until 2 a.m. he was still unsure if it was a boy or a girl. He explained all this on the phone in between learning that it was a boy, asking if it had ten fingers and toes, assuring his wife that he too would be bruised after twenty hours of labour, and repeated insistences to "take care of little one," he had to go. Zosia and I filled the time waiting for the report by queueing for bread, which has doubled in price in the time I have been here. "I never pay attention to prices," Zosia remarked. "You can't go out with less than 30,000 zloties in your purse in case there is something you need. And if I need it, I buy it." She told me they were planning to phase out the hard currency shops early next year.

Friday December 8th
Warsaw

Jacek Gzaputowicz has a new job. He is one of the advisers to the Senate International Commission and seems to have found his place. He looked completely at home in his new office in the parliament, with potted plants, fax machine, two phones and his own, very nice assistant. It makes a change from organising illegal international seminars in churches.

He invited us down, to show us around the parliament. It's a white, airy, elegant building and compared to much of Warsaw's pompous neostalinist architecture, built on a human scale. We sat and watched part of the debate on the prisoners amnesty. Solidarity deputies sit on the "right" in the Sejm, Communists on the "left," Peasants and Democrats in the middle. Mazowiecki, looking worn, and his team sat slightly above it all in a separate box. Radek was in the Secretary's chair looking very young. Votes come up on a kind of cricket score board in orange flashing lights. While we were there four members of the PZPR announced that they were separating from the Communist party and wanted to have connections with other parliamentary clubs. "Dissolving before one's eyes" is the correct expression.

The voting on the Amnesty was touch and go Janusz Onyszkiewicz told us at lunch today. He had been concerned that they wouldn't get the two thirds majority necessary to reject a senate amendment and pass the reform. "Our penal system is extremely severe – no short sentences – only five, six, ten years. And as you might have noticed we have no parliamentary discipline, so each voting is a kind of lottery." A whip system was fiercely rejected in the Solidarity parliamentary group and it requires an 80% majority even to approve a recommendaton on voting, "so everyone is autonomous, and votes as he likes."

The whole atmosphere is still, in parts, one of schoolboys occupying the headmaster's study. When we went to see Minister Hall, for example, at the Council of Ministers, none of the Security guards knew where in the labyrinth of stuffy, carpeted corridors, his office was. And when we found him he was extremely unministerial: a shy, slightly balding man in an ill fitting suit jacket and baggy trousers he was very apologetic about having moved our appointment and gave us far more than the arranged time. (Jan Rokita might learn something.)

While we were waiting in the anteroom for Minister Hall we heard Janek Litynski making an impassioned speech about the nomenclatura working within the cooperative structures. (The cooperatives have a monopoly on the distribution and organisation of most goods and services, especially in agriculture.) "I am very disturbed by the way these old structures are defended. . . ." He gave the example of bosses taking revenge for an agreement reached after a strike by farmers, by refusing to deliver milk. "So citizens go without . . . The economy needs rapid and radical moves. This parliament talks too much about politics and while they do, the Nomenclatura rob the nation of its property."

Onysikiewicz didn't see the Nomenclatura as an insoluble problem. "It's not a block. In 1981 they dug in, closed ranks, they predicted it wouldn't last. Now they know that time is gone. So the only way to survive is to find space in the new situation. Everyone is fighting for himself. They are opportunists and respond to instructions coming from on top. My optimism is based on exploitation of this not very glorious side of human nature – opportunism." Even so, he still felt a "strong force" was essential to crush "this network" in the local elections.

He had just come back from a visit to Britain with Lech Walesa and as usual radiated cheerful good humour. He had resigned as Spokesman of the Trade Union, "because I think my electorate must know I'm speaking as their servant, not in the name of the Trade Union. But they don't want to accept my resignation, so I'm on strike," he smiled. He was quite optimistic about the situation. "People are now quite prepared to accept reforms, provided we do them fast. And prices of some products are actually falling.

There is a basically stable free rate of exchange of the dollar. It will have another jump soon, because we have to change the price of energy. But the situation is much more stable." He had every hope that they would get the aid they needed. And he wasn't too worried about the developments in other East European countries diverting aid from Poland. "East Germany will be looked after by West Germany. Luckily for the Czechs and Hungarians and for us, their economies are in a much better shape. If Romania explodes one day, which is quite likely – *then* there wll be a real problem. Obviously that doesn't mean that we don't wish them to develop democracy; this is something we will have to put up with. I believe Poland is a pivotal country. If things collapse here then the chances they will succeed elsewhere are much smaller."

The key issues of the moment however are: in what form the citizen's committees will develop, what impact this will have on the development of political pluralism; and the connected question of whether there should be a law for political parties or whether a simple Constitutional provision for their existence is enough. Jacek Czaputowicz explained yesterday that Communists were opting for the creation of a restrictive law which included the provision that only those political forces which have *said* they are political parties can elect candidates. The OKP prefer the constitutional option, while Minister Hall and Jacek fall somewhere in beween: a nonrestrictive law to deal with technical questions. "A law provides some recognition," said Jacek.

In fact both polar positions appear to conceal hidden agendas. Those arguing most heatedly for the development of the formal structures of political pluralism – particularly on the Right – are those who feel frustrated by being outside the mainstream and whose own party ideologies do not strike one as very democratic. While the OKP's position seems to allow it to continue an informal domination of the political scene. Onyszkiewicz told us that "the time for political parties has not come yet." However Jacek Czaputowicz told us that those attempting to set up PSR (the prewar peasants' party) were strongly attacked. "They succeeded but everything was done to eliminate them. OKP doesn't want to recognise new parties. It's not in their interest. What we need now is a really democratic election in which we see how influential each group is. I am a bit concerned, especially after the events in Czechoslovakia – that we will no longer be the leaders in reform but the one that conserves the situation in the coming years. It's stupid, now they are members of parliament they would like to stay two years, four years, very happy and important."

It is a paradox that "anticommunism" seems to reproduce the monopolistic tendencies of Communism itself: in the hands of the right, who would replace the ideology of Marxism with that of the Catholic church. And in Solidarity – whose underground informal structures enabled it to survive and challenge Communist rule, but are also what results in elitist and antidemocratic tendencies, now that they are in power.

To complicate matters further the citizens' committees are organising to field their own candidates. Onyszkiewicz hopes this will be under the name "Solidarity," in spite of the Union's possessiveness of that title; and a suggestion has been made that the movement as a whole should consolidate into a single new form of party. This morning a senator in Jacek Czaputowicz's office was arguing strongly against this, saying one hundred senators had signed a petition demanding that each local citizens committee should have autonomy to work in the elections as it wished. Minister Hall also clearly felt this was "not a good idea, it would lead to divisions" and that the committees should continue as "coalitions of different political forces."

It was Janek Litynski, this evening, who gave us the most articulate arguments in favour of the idea, expanding on the proposals he had made two months ago, describing his goal as "saving the mainstream of Solidarity as one 'political organisation'." He thought the term "party" implied a kind of "discipline" that he didn't think the movement needed.

"It could be a democratic system with the definite colour of Solidarity – a practical organisation that is liberal if the situation requires it but also very sensitive to social movements and demands." He compared it to both the Gaullist movement in France, emphasising that the ideology would not be the same; and to American political parties with the whole spectrum of political opinion contained within them. "Because the discussion between Christian Democrats and Social Democrats for example, is ridiculous!" He felt that, because of the political vacuum that had existed in Poland for the last forty years there were "no proper political parties" because movements had not had an opportunity to develop to political maturity in the way that the Greens had in West

Germany for example. Consequently while political parties in the West were arguing about economic policy, the new parties in Poland had no concrete programmes, simply "slogans about national unity." "We are fed up with this and would like to try and form another kind of organisation." "Couldn't that create the same problems that the Democratic party has in the U.S., that its inclusiveness is deceptive. It is too large to respond to the interests of smaller groups. Might not coalitions of smaller parties, that change according to the political currents of the time be more flexible?"

"In Holland it may be coalitions of small parties, but our political tradition *is* Solidarity. I would like to try and save this political tradition. Maybe we will fail . . . but it's a chance for us."

He was able to acknowledge the criticisms of the political opposition without dismissing them as idiots. Though he did feel that the criticisms really arose out of the weakness of the opposition groups' political line and that Solidarity's strength and moral authority was because their line was better. "Of course, an organisation like Solidarity, especially after Martial law can have too big an influence on the situation, maybe some of our critics are right, that we want to use our political influence over a less structured movement . . . I will have to consider this. And of course the role of Walesa is typical of a nondemocratic front. It's a danger, but on the other hand it's the normal political influence of leaders in many parties. He has political sense and up to now his line has led to democracy. Moreover there is a democratic process in parliament – it's not unified, even in the OKP. But we are a strong movement. For example, if Mazowiecki's government were to fail we might still be able to form the next government with a new political line. For the sake of political stability in Poland, I hope Solidarity has the majority in the next parliamentary elections."

"As I said to Adam (Michnik) and Jacek (Kuron), now is the last chance for us to create a political organisation or party. It doesn't matter what you call it, but I don't think it will be possible after six months." He saw three obstacles: firstly that the national citizens' committee simply couldn't make up its mind what to do; secondly that KKW (the Trade Union Executive) still hankered after being both a trade union and a political organisation with influence, and were afraid of competition; and thirdly there were difficulties with the local citizens' committees and their real reluctance to formalise in any way. "You say that *we* are using this undefined organisation to our own ends. But it's not so simple. These people in the local organisations don't want to form a political party. They just want to be a movement. We suggested for example that members of other political parties should not be able to join our clubs, which is a non open way of forming a party of course. People in the local committees were against it. I pointed out that this lack of rules could result in the committees becoming a forum for struggle between various political tendencies – they said 'no, there's no such danger. Those political groups try to get onto our committees and we just kick them out (informally of course). We don't want a political discussion – we have our local problems to resolve and we don't want politicians like that'. Well it's just one step for them to go from rejecting politicians from other parties to rejecting politicians like ourselves, altogether!"

One of the real difficulties was language. Onyszkierwicz told us today, "nobody would identify themselves as a 'politician' it is seen as a betrayal. Such words are contaminated." "People are genuinely afraid of being stamped political," Janek said. "And our political language is very weak. It's strong if you are talking about 'independence', 'punishing the Communists' and so on but we are trying to discuss 'compromise' and not to avoid the term politics but to explain that politics is difficult."

This made it even harder to deal with the extreme right who use clear and uncomplicated language. "I hope the Polish Nation is rational enough not to listen to such bullshit," Janek said. He felt people were becoming increasingly uncomfortable with the antisemitism and beginning to reject it.

In his view the important political struggle in the future would be between a Solidarity mainstream on one hand and the extreme left and extreme Right on the other – particularly the traditional and nationalist Right. "Our main tool against this is our European tendency. We need to organise an alliance with the Czechs and Hungarians. There is now the real possibility of an organised International movement towards Democracy in Eastern and Western Europe."

"Perhaps the new alliance could do something about Romania?" I said half joking.

"Romania! Romania needs some form of international intervention," Janek replied.

Sunday December 10th
West Berlin

Sosza and Sigismund gave T. and I a beautiful farewell dinner to which Janek and Krysza and the dog came. Krysza read my cards and predicted, among other things, a journey. Not so difficult as she knew I was driving to Slovenia – the long way. Neither T. nor I can currently go through Czechoslovakia. By the time I got to Poznan I was so exhausted I was weaving lanes for which I was fined 5000 zloties by another quite friendly policeman.

Elzbieta was very unruffled by being woken at 3 a.m. At breakfast today she told us they have restarted the hunger strike in Gdynia because the referendum is not agreed. She is convinced the whole matter is linked to pressure from the French and West Germans to buy their nuclear technology. However Radek did a poll of the OKP and the majority are against Nuclear power, which bodes well.

T. and I had obtained transit visas to the GDR. And in spite of the GDR embassy warning us about queues and to jump up and down and say we were *not* Polish, something I did not relish, it only took half an hour to cross the Polish frontier. At the crossing from East to West Berlin, the officer just smiled and waved his hand. "Now I *know* the world has come to an end," said T.

Demonstration against Zarnowiec nuclear power station

Against pre-military training

Against Zarnowiec, at Gdynia

Zarnowiec, invading Ministry of Industry committee

Warsaw, WIP graffiti

Pro-choice demonstration

Against PANAM project, Krakow

Warsaw, woman begging

Berlin Wall

Havel monument?

Demonstrators watch themselves on TV

Demonstrators, Prague

Student demonstration, Prague

Graffiti, Bratislava

Part 2

Berlin

Monday December 11th
Berlin

Today I went to a perfectly ordinary political meeting, the kind I have attended countless times in the last 10 years when peace and human rights activists from different European countries sit down and discuss some common project. Only this time, instead of a bunch of frustrated West Europeans discussing how to get representatives of NMS (the Czech Independent Peace Association), WiP, Charter 77, or the East German opposition to the meeting, or wondering which East European city might allow us to meet without deporting us all, we were all sitting in the same room – French, West German, Italian, Dutch, British, East German, Slovene, Polish, Czech and Hungarian. Like my friend Maria in Kakow, I had to keep pinching myself.

Jacek Czaputowicz was asking Barbel Bohley and Ludwig Melhorn (from Neues Forum) about their Polish German situation. He thanked them for their answer to Michnik's letter but felt relationships had got unacceptably bad. "Of course you need border controls, but signs in shops saying 'No Poles', that's unacceptable. And is it necessary for foreign businessmen to have to wait 24 hours before being allowed to cross East Germany and come to Poland? It means that they just give up and go home and we lose business. It's blocking our economy; we need to create a good, quick route through East Germany to Poland. I understand East Germans might not want Poles as competitors in a free market but don't underestimate the danger of nationalism and counter-nationalism."

"Public opinion is being manipulated" Barbel replied "You have to understand. We don't have a new government yet, we have groups of people sitting round a table talking to one another, but the traditional one is in place. The opposition has to demand a transitional government in which it takes part, then the Polish problem can be discussed in another way. And don't try to determine what people think from six banners in Leipzig saying 'Deutschland, unser Vaterland'. It doesn't represent real opinion. I've constantly argued against reunification so far and have had countless letters from people both in the DDR and FRG arguing against reunification and wanting the chance to discuss their own future."

"That's wishful thinking Barbel" Ludwig said. "Yes, there's a consensus in the opposition at the moment that reunification is not desirable and that we need time to talk about democracy, but we have to consider the possibility, and discuss how to get unity within a concept of a European Peace Order. Germany's neighbours are frightened. One condition should be "Don't frighten the neighbours." And Jacek, there is much more to say than was written in that letter, but when you're reproached you have to react immediately. The Polish German border events are the tip of an iceberg. German Polish relations are one of the most central and rotten elements in our history and Poland is in the most serious state of all the countries undergoing revolution."

"Is it a new law?" Jacek asked. "Is it the government stirring up nationalism? Is the opposition too weak to do anything?"

"It's not a law, its a directive from the government, interpreted broadly," Ludwig replied. "Modrow didn't just announce measures against Poles, but in this social psychological atmosphere people are looking for scapegoats and for some of the opposition it is not the main concern. This is also partly your fault. It was very difficult to get in touch with you in the early eighties."

"So is this revenge?" Jacek asked.

"No, of course not." Ludwig replied.

"Some Czechs are frightened of possible reunification." said Hana. "It's difficult to see how this fear can be overcome but at least we have a new government with broad public support."

"The problem here is that on the issue of unification there is a split in all the parties," said a man from *Tageszeitung*. "There is a vacuum and no-one on the left has a 'concept' that can be put forward as an alternative."

An elegant looking woman in a fur hat arrived late. She introduced herself as the Vice Chair of "Democratic Awakening," which was just about to become a political party. "We're trying to gather together socially orientated democrats, the ecologically concerned, those with a religious – not just Christian – orientation, who would like a new type of party. Our main interest in the last weeks has been the German question. The problem has to be Europeanised. We understand people's fears of a big Germany but it's my belief that the fears are groundless. The real problem is not East/West, but North/South, hunger and over population. These are common problems."

One thing that is immediately apparent is that the East German opposition does not come in a neatly labelled package as in Czechoslovakia or Poland. Gerd and Ulricke Poppe gave me a quick summary in the break. I last saw Ulricke six years ago at a peace conference in a protestant church in East Berlin, on my first and last visit to the city. She was part of a woman's peace group at that time.

Now she was representing "Democracy Now" at the round table. "It's a movement not a party," she explained. "There's also a 'Frauen' group, it appears to include a lot of SED women." In addition, Gerd explained, there was the peace and human rights group which he represented; the green party, which was small because so many others had green platforms; "Democracy Awakening," who he thought would probably move to the right, as Christian Democrats; the SDP; a Trotskyist group called "Left Unity" and "Neues Forum," whose growth had been so rapid that they hadn't really had time to formulate a programme. The Round Table consisted of these eight opposition groups and five official parties. "No-one really knows who the government is at the moment." Ulricke said.

"That's why free elections are so important. Our main problem at the moment is to get the government to discuss new laws before putting them into action."

"Socialism is a dirty word," said Gerd, "but all the opposition groups are to the left. All nationalist right-wing groups are very small at present." "What about reunificaton?" I asked. "Jacek told me that a recent poll published in Poland said that 80% in the GDR wanted it."

"We have no way of telling. There haven't been any proper polls so I don't know how he gets the figure. One was done in Leipzig by a youth organisation, which said 48%." "I don't understand why, as you all seem to be friends and have very similar demands, you aren't in some kind of coalition?"

"We've had 40 years of socialist unity. What we need is some pluralism," Gerd replied. "In an election we will probably work together."

Erich (Rathfelder) got home exhausted and late. Too much news (although the nice thing about staying with the Foreign Editor of *Tageszeitung* is that one gets to hear it). Husak has resigned and Havel has been nominated for President. Jiri Dienstbier is Foreign Minister. Thousands are demonstrating in the streets in Prague and the Bulgarians are demanding free elections. Meanwhile the demonstrations in Leipzig are growing nastier. He feels quite worried by what is going on.

"This discovery of corruption in the leadership has taken away the sense of being a GDR citizen. Nationalism replaces this." Hence the increasing number of banners saying "Deutschland unser Vaterland." "There isn't an equivalent in the opposition leadership to Havel. Many of the major figures had to leave, the party is falling apart like a house of cards, and now there is a political vacuum. Two thousand East Germans are still leaving every day," Erich remarked, "West Germany will have to help in one way or the other, either housing them here or making a massive injection of aid and recognising their citizenship there."

"And the Soviet Union is going to open its borders on 1st January," Carol, his American wife added, "so we can expect a massive influx of Russians as well." Feelings were already running high in the refugee camps. "The city has said that only those with first degree relatives can stay in West Berlin, the rest have to go to West Germany." "And the response?" "The East Germans want the Poles kicked out, all 50,000 of them." Carol grinned. "My view is that there are two choices, you can look at it as a great opportunity – start learning five new languages now – imagine the great Russian bars! Or you can get out."

"You know, for the first time today I sensed the 'power' relations, whose city this is" said Erich. The four powers have had their first meeting for God knows how long, and after posing for photos, had run off into the sunset, leaving a press spokesperson to say they had discussed airplane schedules, and communication in Berlin, Oh, and "the German question". But he gave nothing away. Erich had interviewed a high ranking Soviet official, "It's their city: the Soviets and the Americans." "The Soviet explained to me that there are limits. You can only go so far as our American friends agree." The limits are no unification. Erich predicts a kind of anger developing: "Everyone else is allowed self determination, but not us, 'Versailles Verdicht', people feel they are being punished."

Tuesday December 12th
Berlin

"Lenin's monument is coming down in Nowa Huta. The city authorities say its for 'restoration' ". I read in the *Taz* this morning. When they took down Felix Dzierzynski in Warsaw a few weeks ago it fell to pieces, and everyone cheered. I have the feeling however that Lenin may be of tougher material.

"Strange how my country is becoming completely politically invisible." T. remarked as he looked at the paper. "When Bulgaria announces free polls, it's front page news. When Croatia does, it's a small item on Page three. We only make the front page when people are killed." "I suppose people don't see Yugoslavia as so undemocratic as the rest." I said. He smiled, ruefully. "No, and mass protests in Serbia two years ago succeeded in *installing* an authoritarian, Stalinist leader."

Lotte Templin and Peter Rossmann (editor of *Across Frontiers*) came round mid morning to take us over to East Berlin. Lotte has only been allowed back herself for the last month. We took the U-Bahn to Friedrichstrasse. It still looks like a public toilet, but at least it's a more cheerful one and the queues through the booths were moving rapidly. The fresh faced officer took T.'s passport with a smile and then held on to it. The booths are designed to produce anxiety – a mirror above your head angled so that the officer can see you front and back – a high counter shields all but his head so it is not possible to see whether he is reading your name on a list or doing the crossword. In this case however, he was clearly using three separate phones. Our queue was no longer moving rapidly. Suddenly an officer appeared in the eastern doorway of the booth, grasped T. firmly by both arms and pushed him back, past the rest of us, flattening ourselves against the wall, and out onto the western side. The officer was now staring at my passport and had begun on the phonecalls. The man with a Bundesrepublik passport and a blonde woman in the queue beside him, eyed me uncertainly. Who, after all, in these days was not allowed into the DDR? The second officer appeared again as if by magic at the eastern door. The same firm grasp as if I might suddenly try to escape Eastwards. I was pushed beyond the metal barrier dividing border area from U-Bahn and my passport returned. "You may not cross . . . No, we don't have to give the reason." It could have been six years ago, the last time I tried, except the feelings of frustration and bewilderment are greater.

So we spent the afternoon window-shopping on Kurfurstendamm. After three months in Poland I have at least a small sense of what it must feel like to come here from the East. It looked like fairyland. Every tree bejewelled with Christmas lights, shops bursting with fancy goods. I found myself quite transfixed by a display of moving, furry toys in the windows of Ka-De-We.

Erich couldn't believe it. We had rung him in the afternoon and he had put it in the paper. "They must be working from old lists." If it was any comfort, even Gorbachev's adviser on German affairs had been refused a visa at one point when he had upset Honecker by saying "independent movements were a good thing." "Yes, but Honecker's now arrested on criminal charges!" "Well, they'll read about it in the *Taz* and that will have an effect."

Party papers stop getting money in the GDR after the 1st January. Springer press is already buying in and *Tageszeitung* is looking as well. "We thought of calling it '*Trabi Taz*' " Erich said. "Only East German friends said that it would be discriminatory. One good thing about unification means that it allows *Taz* to expand!" He joked. "Do you know that the *Leipziger Zeitung* had 150 editors! 150! When at most it needed six. They were all working for the government of course."

Regarding getting into Czechoslovakia, he suggested we rang Mr Dienstbier, the new Foreign Minister. After all, it was because of attending a seminar with him and other Charter 77 members, that we were expelled last year. Did we know that he had to spend the first two days of his new job doing his old one, stoking fires for two large apartment buildings, because there was no-one to replace him?

Wednesday December 13th
Berlin

We went to the Polish market this morning, it occupies the corner of a bleak, muddy open space near Checkpoint Charlie. The vendors cluster in the relative shelter of the overhead railway. Young men in leather jackets hold out single bottles of Cognac and boxes of Marlboros. Pale young women sell fur hats, cheap china and glass. There are older people as well, each with a small pile of goods, some looking like personal possessions, heaped onto plastic carrier bags laid on the ground. There is very little food. The buyers are mostly Turkish women, one minority selling to another. The market began when the Poles first got freedom to travel. They can come to Berlin for 30 days, without a visa, and initially they were selling anything they could carry, often buying in East Berlin and bringing it over. That is stopped now. Customs officers are heavy on foodstuffs, but with 25,000 people coming in and out every day, there is little else they can do. The street vendors wanted the market suppressed but the City Council is currently Polish-friendly. *Tageszeitung* produces a Polish language newspaper and sees the market as a good sign of exchange between East and West, an aspect of freedom to travel which should be respected. T. found it depressing and humiliating. "This is an achievement of Communism: to turn the misery produced by the system into something very personal and intimate. It's not that they are starving, it's that they are reduced to a state in which they are prepared to sell their personal belongings, even when it is not necessary for their survival."

So we turned away and walked along the wall. It has always been a bizarre and ugly place. It is still bizarre but has acquired the atmosphere of a kind of citizens' adventure playground. The joggers, cyclists and women pushing baby carriages along the muddy track beside the wall all look happy. We bought Gluhwein from one of the numerous booths, and in a short walk passed three elderly people gazing excitedly through a hole at a mallet lying in the mud on the other side; a man lifting up his spaniel to look through a crack; four Japanese students doing a song and dance routine to disco music, waving U.S. flags to the cheers of an admiring audience; a middle-aged woman in beige trying to remove a piece of metal with a hacksaw; some smartly dressed Americans looking like off-duty diplomats who were each solemnly chipping off their own bit of wall, and another man, in beautifully tailored navy blue coat, painting the wall with violet paint. All this, to the 'chink chink' sound of the professional chippers – men and boys in goggles and tracksuits with plastic bags in which a large number of painted fragments were carefully gathered. Similar fragments were being sold in the booths across the way at DM 5.00 for three. Perhaps the price will rise as the volume of wall available decreases. One could also buy T-shirts showing 'GorBATchev' opening the Brandenburg gate and "ICH WAR DABEI".

Erich told us at dinner this evening that the East German police had had serious discussions with East German artists on how to paint their side of the wall. They have offered cars, material and any assistance needed, provided that the painting meets the required aesthetic criteria. Mostly, we talked about the role of the Soviet troops in the current crisis. Willy Brandt was on television today saying that Soviet troops ordered the Volksarmee back into barracks on 9th October during the Leipzig demonstration and prevented them from attacking the crowd. When asked whether this was true Brandt answered "Man sagt nichts wenn man nicht genau weiss." Carol added that on the night of 9th November in Berlin, when the wall came down, the Soviet Commander had phoned to the US Commander and each had agreed that from their points of view, everything in their own sectors was under control. Whereas there are rumours from Prague that the army threatened a coup d'etat to force Adamec to appoint a Minister of Defence to their liking and that they even surrounded the city. It came to nothing, perhaps beause of Soviet pressure? "Why are the Czech military asking for the Russians to leave?" said Erich. "So, my idea is that they should go home, via Romania. Romania," he gestured with his hand across his throat, "that will be a blood bath unless someone has the sense to stage a coup d'etat."

Thursday December 14th
Berlin

Peter and Lotte had realised in 10 minutes that we weren't coming. They had protested to some party big-wig who had made appropriate noises of distress. Gerd had complained as well, saying if the situation wasn't changed it would be an issue for the Round Table. Both T. and I felt rather honoured at this. We were asked to try again to see if any of this had taken effect.

It had worked for me but not for T. Perhaps because the *Taz* called him a "Slovakian" rather than a "Slovene" intellectual, or because the authorities are slightly more worried about offending the British than the Yugoslav governments. Anyway, T. said he would wander round bookshops, so I went over with Peter.

Berlin, the "Hauptstadt" of the DDR is still a grey, gloomy city, particularly on a cold wet December afternoon. Even the primary colours on the doors and windows of the new, post-modernist buildings in the centre don't relieve it. "They spent all this money on Berlin for the 750th Anniversary celebrations. To the detriment of other cities of course." Peter remarked. What has changed however, is the people. It's hard to define but the faces in the street had an energy and cheerfulness I don't associate with city workers, either here or in London . The woman changing my compulsory DM20 was all smiles and goodwill . . .

Goodwill also oozed from government spokesperson Wolfgang Meyer and his colleague at an afternoon press conference. Two pale faced, grey suited men in an ugly panelled room; every question however aggressive was greeted with a friendly smile: "A commission was being formed to investigate the theft of socialist property." The Stasi (secret police) were being dissolved and their property being used for charitable purposes. Wandlitz (the luxurious living quarters for party leaders) would become a rehabilitation centre for handicapped children on February 1st. "I rang up the Stasi today to ask what would happen to their employees," said the man from the *Financial Times*, "they said they couldn't answer as they were being dissolved."

"The opposition has said you are incapable of governing and has demanded a role in government," another journalist asked. "This government has a mandate and a clear programe. Of course there are some groups trying to interfere and disrupt the process of government. I can only appeal for non violence and that they allow us to do our job."

It felt like the last gasp. The answers were vague, evasive and non specific, full of those useful non-commital phrases: A "contractual arrangement" with the FRG was being considered. This was not the same as a confederation. A security service of some kind was needed, they had the same security needs as everyone. No, Wolfgang's colleague, whose name I didn't catch, was not a Stalinist, just a "tough man." (Apparently someone had been parading outside his office with a placard saying "The last Stalinist"). "Heavy industry could no longer be subsidised at the expense of people's living standards and ecological damage must be reversed." "Who's responsible for the damage?" "We're looking into this." "Of course we 'greet' the developments in Czechoslovakia." New ideas? "Joint ventures are not a miracle weapon, lessons must be learnt from the last 40 years."

In the window of a small exhibition centre on Alexanderplatz, someone had hung a long strip of kitchen towel saying "The DDR is the sum total of everything that could have been avoided."

Alexanderplatz resembles one of Britain's nastier 60's shopping centres, only worse because there is more concrete wasteland and less shops. The exhibition was housed in one of the tent-like structures tethered to the communications tower that features as a symbol of technological advance on so many East Berlin postcards. A collecton of photographs, banners, hangings and placards were placed quite haphazardly around a number of booths, one for each of the opposition groups. "I stand behind any government that doesn't stand in front of me," "Without women nothing happens." Leaflets, explaining the group positions were in short supply so you had to stand and read the statements pinned up. What struck me was how similar they all sounded, demanding a democratic, ecologically sound future with human rights and social justice. Erich remarked yesterday that the Communists are more Green than the West German Greens.

Peter is a good companion but terrible guide, complaining bitterly that European cities don't work on a grid, like American ones. We got lost in the short distance between Alexanderplatz and the Neues Forum office. When we arrived the place seemed quite unprepossessing for one of the centres of an enormous opposition movement. Yellow room, badly lit, some tables covered with duplicated sheets, a desk and two tired looking men on the phone and that was it. Barbel was at home and told us to come round.

A pleasant looking man clutching a bundle of papers opened the door, an engineer working on the electoral system. "No, I'm not a lawyer, I know how to make systems work." The initial idea, he explained, was to only have individuals, no parties. They had compromised on that. Parties will now be allowed. "All parties are corrupt," Barbel said emphatically, "we have enough parties to cover the whole political spectrum. What we don't have is a politically conscious public, and forming parties won't create it. It's created by a process of democratic discussion."

Barbel's apartment is light, with bare walls, a sculpture of a pregnant woman on the piano, china cupboard and numerous books. We sat round her table; the engineer, Peter, myself, and another English woman – a friend of Barbels, Margaret, and a non stop succession of visitors. Barbel talks in a rapid, soft, intense manner, interrupting herself to answer the phone and make coffee repeatedly for everyone. The engineer explained that Neues Forum would field candidates in the election but unlike the political parties, they would be directly accountable to, and recallable by, the electorate. "The elections would be in May, too late for the country, too soon for any of the groups, official parties or otherwise, but until the elections, we have no legitimate government," the engineer explained.

"Does Neues Forum have an ideology? A common platform?"

"Ideologies are the last thing we want," Barbel said.

"They are the only ones who don't mention Socialism and probably the only ones who really believe in it," Margaret said.

"Socialism," Barbel said, "we have to get away from these concepts. People here understand Socialism as meaning oppression, exploitation, having no voice. What people want here is Western consumer goods. They aren't capable of renouncing it and how can you blame them? How can I stand up and ask people to tolerate conditions like this. I went to England, the streets here were kaput, I return, the streets are kaput. People in Leipzig suffer appalling pollution and their children are sick. Meanwhile, they go to the West and see there is plenty of democracy there, Socialism is kaput." She sounded upset. "People won't care about ecology before they have clean living conditions themselves. In Neues Forum we simply say, people may have democracy but run towards it with open eyes."

"So why do the German opposition still talk about Socialism when the Polish opposition, for example, rejected it?"

"We still think it's the better Germany. We have grown up with the idea that the other side are the evil ones, Capitalists, Nazis."

"The Germans are used to believing their masters," said the engineer, "whereas for hundreds of years the Poles . . ."

"No," disagreed Barbel, "that's not it. The Germans have much on their conscience. Many people believed it served us right . . ."

We drank more coffee. I had brought Christmas biscuits from West Berlin. "Beautiful Capitalism," laughed Barbel, "one must queue for hours for these," she pointed to the chocolate Father Christmas wrapped in silver paper. "Either it's really bad or it's not. Sometimes everything seems normal. I go to Alexanderplatz to shop, the next minute it's crazy." She told us how she had received death threats, "So have some Neues Forum people in Schwerin," said the engineer.

"Well, if God wants it, at least I'll have a good funeral. The police say they can't do anything. For years they've been watching me and now they can't protect me."

She was opening post. Someone had sent a news magazine with a page of photos of those most responsible for the wall coming down. Hers was included. The irony is that she was totally against it being opened. "There is nothing good about it. I said at the time, the government have gone mad, and of course I've been attacked. But it was completely crazy. 2,000 people are leaving every day! 2,000! They should have made a good travel law, giving citizens complete freedom to travel and so much money. And the Western media were part of the whole foul business. Before, the population was divided between those who stay and those who go. Now it's between those who do and don't want unification." She shook her head. "Every political decision the government makes increases the catastrophe. From the 1st January the West Germans don't have to change money."

"And what Poles buy up will be nothing compared to what West Germans do," said Peter.

"What is happening here is a chance for the world but we can't manage to realise it. In 1968 there was a chance for socialism. Not now, we can't get people enthusiastic about it," Barbel continued.

"I'm a socialist," said Peter.

"So why don't you create it, why do you expect us to create it when you can't do it yourselves?"

"Leftists from the Federal Republic," the engineer came in, "they travel from one revolution to the other, Nicaragua, Vietnam, Chile, and now the DDR, while things in their own country remain bad."

"I have a real fear," Barbel went on, "that it will be East and West against the third world. No one thinks about these problems. They are just completely focused on 'the German problem' ".

One of the tired looking men had arrived from the Neues Forum office. "You've got it cosy," he remarked, pulling off his coat and sitting down. Someone made more coffee. The engineer was telling me he had only been back one month, having been forced to leave the DDR eleven years ago. He wanted to found an ecological centre in Schwerin. There were many castles and buildings going cheaply as the State sold its property.

"One good thing about an increase in democracy here was that it included the possibility of democratising the economy." He explained, "In West Germany we see a tendency in the opposite direction. The EEC has its Politbureau in Brussels and its Parliament, as useless as the Volkskammer in Strasbourg." I noticed he used the past tense. There is the feeling that these people have almost resigned themselves to the inevitable. Barbel says "Kohl is coming on Tuesday so you can expect 500,000 roaring for unification."

The conversation drifted onto Gysi, "a good man in the wrong party," the engineer said.

"Good that he is Jewish, he understands facism," said someone else. "I think he's trying to save the SED because he believes if it collapses right wing groups will fill the vacuum."

"What will happen to the 'Party'?" I asked.

"It may dissolve. At least they are not going to wage civil war on us," the engineer replied, "we can save something."

"What is worth saving?"

"The feeling of being more communal," he said thoughtfully, "But perhaps this common feeling grows out of resistance to oppression and disappears when repression disappears. The best thing to save would be to keep political control over the economy, not the other way around: economy controlling politics as you have in the West."

It was dark and wet walking to the subway. There are still official placards up in Rosa Luxembourg Plaza quoting her writing: "The Enemy is at home."

Prague

Monday December 18th
Prague

Phoning Mr Dienstbier worked. In spite of the nasty blemish on T.'s passport, they permitted us to cross the frontier, still heavily fortified with two rows of wire mesh and watch towers, plus a welcoming notice on the Czech side reminding us that "Our power resides in the unity and friendship of Socialist countries." Streams of Trabants were going in the other direction. Czechoslovakia is still a faster route to the West because of the queues from East to West Germany. I have the sensation that one half of East Europe is day tripping in the other. None of these carried luggage.

Czechoslovakia has Havel fever, every shop, every telegraph post in the small towns through which we drove on the way here, displayed his poster and the atmosphere in Prague is one of delirious excitement. Shops are open, businesses function, but there is a sensation of the whole city being on holiday and walking about in the street. Small crowds are gathered everywhere: in the main square, queuing to sign a petition endorsing Havel's nomination; around every large shop window, all of which have turned into impromptu notice boards. Czechs seem particularly fond of rhyming slogans: "Konec Vlady, jedne strany" (An end to one party rule), "Odvonici vcele, podvonici v cele" (Committee to the front, Vanguard to the cells). The University is still on strike as only four of its demands have been met.

Walking back to the hotel we stumbled into another crowd. This time of some 400 women and children holding Chinese lanterns and balloons outside the Town Hall. A smartly dressed man of about 40 appeared to be shouting something from the town hall steps, brightly lit by TV cameras but quite inaudible. The crowd was restive. "We're Prague mothers," a woman in a red anorak, with an infant in her arms explained to me. "We're all in the Civic Forum and we came to ask the Mayor about our living conditions because they are no good: the air, the water, it's all bad for us, for our children. This Mayor now, he knew we were coming and he hasn't prepared for us at all, no microphone, nothing." "Who is the Mayor?" a banner asked.

Simecka's wife told us that he was staying in Prague, no phone, so we walked the two blocks from our hotel, joining a young student on the stairs outside the apartment. A good looking, dark haired woman opened the door, welcoming us all in as if expected guests. "The Minister of Information has just left, he is very miserable," she remarked in French without waiting for introductions. Simecka was sitting in the living room next to an elderly lady in a nylon housecoat who spoke to us in German. Simecka spoke English and while the dark haired woman poured wine, both complained at the "paradox of the revolution," leaving no-one any time to sit and have coffee and discuss things for hours, as they used to. "In some ways it was better in the old times. All our friends are coming back to Prague, people I haven't seen for twenty years – and when we meet it's for five minutes and there is no emotion. When I saw Havel, who is my best friend, last week in Bratislava, it was for half an hour. He listened to me with one ear, someone else with the other and wrote notes at the same time. It's not the life he wanted but we have to do it."

It seems that what is making the Minister of Information unhappy is that he is a philosopher: a dissident, accustomed for the last twenty years to depend on his own resources – like home-made wine and sausages. "Now he has to ride in a large black car, which he hates. He took his sausages to work with him for the first few days," Simecka told us. "Our Foreign Minister rang me up and asked me where I would like to be ambassador – London, Washington, he offered me thirty places. I turned it down. My wife and I, being anglophiles it might have been nice to be ambassador to London, but for twenty years I've dreamed of this freedom, time to write and think, now I have it . . . We are a very small group and in some ways totally unprepared for the speed – three days! The Party committed suicide. There aren't enough of us to around and we haven't the necessary skills. We are used to circulating underground journals, not printing a newspaper for millions. So we will have to collaborate."

The young student had retreated to another room to discuss something with our hostess. "This new generation are going to govern in ten years and this time is vital for them. That's why I laughed when the rectors say they shouldn't be on strike. Nothing could be more important. The '68 generation is in one sense morally broken. The issues facing us in the future are moral, not existential. This is a moral revolution, we have coffee and bread, it's not like Poland, about economics. It's against the lie."

We arranged an appointment for Wednesday and went out into the street. In a shop window a television set was playing films of 1968 and November 17th this year. A crowd stood around the window, solemnly watching their own history as they themselves created it.

Tuesday, December 19th
Prague, 4 p.m.

In the fairy tales I read as a child, the "good man", woodcutter, travelling minstrel or whatever, after many trials and tribulations and tests of his virtues and courage, always came out on top. The evil king was defeated and the citizens, relieved of their oppressors, "rejoiced". I always found this hard to believe, experience didn't bear it out, besides which, I could never really picture what "rejoicing citizens" would look like. Now I know. Today the students are demonstrating their support for Havel, the Good Man, wrongfully imprisoned and now almost certain to be given a fairy tale castle of his own. The street party has been going on since I woke up to a crowd of students marching past the hotel. The main concentration is in Wenceslas Square, under the Parliament but tentacles stretch, amoeba like, throughout the city. You run the risk at any point of being accosted by one group in mediaeval armour, or another dressed up as riot police. Greenpeace, always with an eye for a good position, have parked their buses across the bottom of Wencelas Square and the whole of Prague seems to have adorned themselves with their yellow stickers, saying "Be active today, not radioactive tomorrow." Outside the Civic Forum office, situated in what was once the offices of the Soviet Czech Friendship Association, at regular intervals, the crowds swirl into the small square. They shout for Havel and go on shouting untl he appears smiling on a balcony and waves. Then they swirl out again and there is relative quiet until another crowd builds up with the same demand. T. and I retreated into the Aurora Gallery, which also serves as a Civic Forum office, to look for Jan Urban, from Charter 77. We had rung him yesterday saying that, having been arrested and deported from his apartment last summer it would be nice to talk to him for a little longer, and he invited us down. "We are trying to get organised," he said, a tall thin bony man in an anorak, standing amongst piles of boxes and a circle of envelope stuffers, and looking slightly despairing. "We don't want to be a vertical hierarchical structure. We would like to be a horizontal grouping of local groups, solving local problems and consulting on nationwide issues," he explained, pulling up a chair, "But we desperately need a nationwide information structure just to be able to organise things." The problem was the speed with which everything had occurred. No-one had predicted it. After the trigger of the student demonstration on 17th November, brutally supressed by the police, and the ensuing student's strike, the theatres immediately became nvolved. Theatres have always played a key role in the Czech opposition. "Fortunately, this immediately gave us a net, a structure to the uprising. It wasn't like the GDR, a big mass movement wthout a structure. We were able to make immediate contact with each other in different states. The other important thing is that it grew everywhere at once. There is still a feeling that we haven't touched the system yet, only cut one head of the dragon, and that's not enough, as every fairy tale says." He saw the main problem as abolishing the political structures inside the police and army. "Article 4 on the leading role of the party has already been abolished, so there is no legal ground for political organisations within the army or security forces. There's an emergency congress of the Communist Party tomorrow which will probably overthrow the old apparatus, but we don't know how deep it will go." They also had to somehow get through the period up to free elections, in the middle of next year. "No one effectively controls the situation. The Communist Party leadership is formed from unknown people who don't even control their own party; the government doesn't control the country, nor does the opposition, and parliament is blocking everything. So the only working structures are the state police, which is very dangerous. We're trying to organise a round table of all political forces: those in the Civic Forum and the Public against Violence (the equivalent opposition umbrella group in Slovakia), and all the new parties, as a kind of emergency cabinet. Hopefully we will have a president elected by the end of the year which should calm down the situation." As for the Communist Party, "it might try the Hungarian route, but in Hungary it's a Hungarian party. Here it's completely based on a false interpretation of 1968 and all those lies. Their position is very difficult. The young Communists are so radical that even in Civic Forum we are trying to slow them down, they could blow up the whole party, which isn't the best solution. If it did collapse, the scene would be free, there would be no need for a united coalition. There are about 20 parties already, you can see the posters everywhere but its impossible to tell if they have 5 members or 500. Charter 77 will stay a human rights movement. It's very probable that the abuse of human rights will continue from the other side, so we are here to defend the rights of the former state policemen against nondemocratic elements in society. People just don't believe it, but it's true."

Jan had to go to answer a hundred messages. So now we are sitting in the cafe downstairs while a class reunion takes place around us. Vit Horejs, a film maker from New York, left Czechoslovakia 20 years ago. He was a friend of Urban's at university and now sits talking to other old friends and classmates: Daniel Kumermann who is in the process of reviving a genuine scouting movement, Hutka the musician, now planning to come back for good. Daniel and T. are discussing the possibility of a Czech/Slovene federation. They insist they are joking. "But it's viable," Daniel says, "it would open a sea for us." "Slovenia is culturally much closer to Czechoslovakia than Serbia," adds T. "And of course it would include Austria, our old ruler," Daniel continues; "The serious point is that either we manage to join the EEC and be on the outer flank or we make things viable among ourselves."

I have been reading through the documentation of Civic Forum, thoughtfully duplicated in large quantities in English. Civic Forum seem to have an eye to the outside world that the GDR opposition groups do not. There is a horrifying eyewitness account of the November 17th demonstration, detailed position statements made day by day by the Civic Forum and the Public Against Violence. What comes over above all is the dgnity and humanity of this revolution, the calls for transformation rather than revenge. Reading the draft Constitution I find myself slightly jealous. We could do with something like this at home. "Human and civil rights and freedoms are inalienable, inviolable and sovereign. All rights and freedoms following from international legal documents . . . are guaranteed to their full extent." "What is not forbidden is permitted". "Everyone may claim his rights and if he does not find any other legal route, then the Constitution applies directly and everyone can appeal to the Constitutional Court to have his rights protected."

Of course it would be nice to see the use of a more inclusive pronoun, and the rights of sexual minorities as well as women and children spelt out, but it's hard to imagine Mrs Thatcher introducing a constitutional obligation to protect the environment, or enshrining in such a document, peoples' rights to "self governing local communities where citizens determine their local affairs themselves," or the exercise of power by ". . . popular referendums"; or the right to protection against all decisions of state rule and administration by means of an independent judiciary"; or the "exclusive state ownership of raw materials, water and energy resources, the means of rail and air transportation and the postal system and telecommunications." She would approve of the limitations of rights "in the interest of national security" of course. This term, undefined as always, leaves me uneasy, as do references to "defence of" and "love of homeland," But perhaps the danger of national chauvinism is avoided here by the constitutional right to conscientious objection and alternative service and the statement that relations between people are also governed by the following principles: "democracy, humanness, love of truth." "Truth." That word again.

9.00 p.m.

Erich was right. There is going to be a blood bath in Romania. It's odd how some moments print themselves indelibly in your mind. We were sitting in the high ceilinged, Victorian white office of Petr Pithardt, Spokesperson for the Civic Forum. He was at one end working through correspondence, one ear glued to a portable radio covering the debate in parliament. Jana Petrova, one of the spokespersons for NMS sat opposite us, explaining their role in the new situation and the fact that the official Communist sponsored Peace Council, previously so hostile, was now falling over itself to co-operate with them. It was supporting the release of political prisoners, the idea of a European Citizens Assembly and helping to draft a new military law. Then Daniel came in and said that the Romanian army had started shooting people, thousands are possibly dead already at a place called Timisoara. Outside, the shouting for Havel was rising in a steady crescendo. I felt cold and tired and helpless, the "Prague euphoria" suddenly drained away. Jana went off to phone Czech TV with a statement.

Here, at least, things were progressing by constitutional means. Pithardt told us the debate had reached a crucial point. "They are voting on whether to use a secret ballot to elect the president." "How do you think it will go?" "Impossible to tell." A short stocky man with greying hair and beard, he smiled; "Unfortunately it's going to be decided by secret ballot."

"Is Civic Forum going to become a political party?" I asked. "We've redefined our organisation at least 8 times to deal with the developing situation, but one thing has been clear from the beginning. We are not going to be a political party, not only in the classical sense, but in any sense. At a critical point, when we could have dictated the government of our choice, we proposed two Communists and four candidates from other parties. The break-up of this totalitarian regime is the priority, not our own representation." "And in the future?"

"We will suggest and support candidates of other parties, especially the newly founded ones that are weak. We will have our own candidates but so far we've avoided the formulation of a 'candidate from Civic Forum' and said 'a candidate supported by Civic Forum'." He didn't think Civic Forum would disappear after the elections. "Many people will stay outside the political parties. It will be needed for them and the new parties as a kind of guarantee of political culture." He was surprised that so far they hadn't paid their usual "price": "The worsening of relations between Czechs and Slovaks, as has happened at every period of sudden change; '39, '47, '68 . . ." Urban this morning had felt there was a problem of some "irrational nationalist sentiments arising," because of Dubcek's candidacy for the presidency. Pithardt agreed, "Dubcek is a sensitive man, he's been isolated for a long time and it's not easy to deal with him. He has an immense need, not for power but visible satisfaction, and it's not only for him, but all Slovakia. That could lead to a certain reversal."

"Is there any danger from the Soviet Union?" I asked.

"None at all!" He replied. "Czechoslovakia has a certain charisma." Jana Petrova said. "We can do without too much economic help and don't have a problem with nationalism as in Germany or with cultural backwardness, as in the Soviet Union. Thanks to our cultural and historical traditions, I think we're in the best position in Eastern Europe."

Charisma is perhaps the right word. It is helped by the fact that all these events take place against the theatrical backdrop of this extraordinarily beautiful city. The castle looms over you in one direction, the parliament in another, and in between, winding mediaeval streets bring you to a swan-filled river. Meanwhile, the nightly press conferences are held in a real theatre, "The Magic Lantern." Tonight the key player was Havel himself, who began by apologising for the fact that his lack of availability was making the journalists fight amongst themselves.

What to make of this modest man who read his television speech from the page last week because he doesn't like "the swindle" of the teleprompt; who would be "very happy when this popularity fades because it is slightly complicating my work"; and who very much doubts that after a free election any political force would nominate him for a five year period. He had none of the slickness of a professional politician. Very blond, tired, but better looking than his photos, he leant forward earnestly to the microphones. "I have never started or carried out any campaign. If someone wants me as President they will have to campaign for that. Who it is will depend on the people. I am not attempting to 'compete' in or 'win' the election." He refused to be drawn on Dubcek, insisting that he would not allow a wedge to be driven between them, they were in frequent contact and what was at stake was "not he or I but the relationship between our two nations. Some wishes for the future are best fulfilled if not discussed while maturing." And he insisted that the task of a "working President," elected for 6 months, was to guarantee the taking place of free elections in a proper manner, treating everyone as if they had the same rights. His main concern was to have elections without "intrigue, underhand methods or plagued by personal ambition. We want to preserve the image of an uprising of purity against soil and dirtiness." As to what the Communist party should do, it was not for him to say, but since he was asked, "if I were a Communist I would attempt to change the party as speedily as possible into a modern party that can participate as an equal amongst equals in a pluralistic political system. I would be happy if they became a partner with whom one could negotiate and work together and which did not consider all those who are not its members as inferior people." Would he have joined a "reform minded Swedish type Communist party" if it had existed 2 years ago? "I have never been a member of any political party and will never become one . . . my personal idea is that in the future personalities should play an increasingly large role and political parties should be reduced to the role of mere clubs in which political personalities have the opportunity to present themselves to the public. Political parties should not directly participate in the 'powers that be'. That is one of the methods by which those powers become anonymous. The only way of saving this civilisation is to make it capable of freeing a specific individual human personality from the manipulation of all the mega structures which modern man has created and now threaten to destroy him."

But the press were not ready to abandon political parties. What were the hopes for a "real left wing party?" "Words like left and right, in our country and within its language, have lost connection with their original meaning and don't coincide with the meaning they have in other countries." "And what will you say to Mr Gorbachev?" "If I were President and had the opportunity to speak to him, I would say what I have said to the staff of the Central Committee of the Communist Party of the Soviet Union: The Soviet Union has nothing to fear from Czechoslovakia, even if the word socialist disappears from its name, but they should be more fearful of some countries, like Romania, that still keep the word."

Rude Pravo is still not happy with Mr. Havel. After 20 years of insults and libel, the Civic Forum asked them to publish an apology, an official biography, and a basic proclamation from Charter 77. Its response was somewhat half-hearted; an apology to a number of unspecified people, the Charter text, but no biography. The official youth daly has now issued a stinging attack saying

X – my publisher lost! 2 pages of prog! I have them if you're interested XX L.

Rude Pravo should conduct an extensive analysis of its conduct in the last 20 years and stop publishing people who had compromised themselves.

Outside, the crowds still stood around the TV monitors. Opposite the parliament young men stood waving flags and shouting to passing cars who tooted in return. In Wenceslas Square people had lit candles around photos of Jan Palach and Masaryk. "We are Masaryk's children" someone had scrawled at the subway entrance. too soon after Martial law to have "changed the generation". "Our enthusiasm was 7–8 years ago – people are tired and they reember. In Czechoslovakia they are completely new, and convinced of what they are doing."

Simecka described how the "Public against Violence" had sprung up completely "spontaneously" – "not directed by anyone – young people, painters, actors, waiters. I had this feeling: now is the moment, you must direct it all, then I saw it was not needed. People were working with all the old ideas that we had in the years before. . . . And after one or two weeks there were factory committees and workers with us. It was the dream of the students of the sixties in Germany but they didn't manage it."

"I must say this is not a normal political culture. It is a revolutionary culture. And in all revolutions you can have informal structures, built without democratic rule, just who came first, and who was there . . . What we must do is build a normal political culture. I said to them you must for example get groups from Slovakia together and elect a leadership in a normal democratic way. In all revolutions known in history there is the danger of little dictators . . ." He didn't feel the danger was so great. Partly because of the tradition of Charter 77 and the moral authority of people like Havel and partly because he did not see the Civic Forum and Public against Violence continuing as formal political organisations but more as informal movements at community level, alongside other movements, organisations and political parties. He envisaged a multiparty democracy. "We don't want one great organisation, we have had terrble experience with this National popular front in the past, as a tool of the Communists. There will be a natural differentiation in this civic movement. I'm a little sceptical that this terrible political engagement in civic society can continue for a long period. Personally I think it's better to build a State where not everyone is interested in Politics."

As for the Communist party, there was no chance of a revitalisation of old ideas, but he hoped its members would stay and work. "Three generations of intellectual potential have been smashed in Czechoslovakia – during the war, '44–48, and after '68 . . . I hope I won't be a witness to another such destruction. The intellectual potential of this nation is not so great that we have the luxury of smashing a generation every 20 years."

"And what will you do?" I asked.

"I will live as I have been living all these years as a free writer".

We spent the afternoon walking around Bratislava, the lovely old town, golden in unseasonal sunshine. There were freshly painted posters pinned up – "In Romania they are shooting people – We protest peacefully." As in Prague doors and windows were covered with leaflets while one entire square was walled in with strikingly painted hoardings. "Europe needs a healthy heart," "Dialogue not Violence," "Who is burning the Archives?" – each slogan dramatically illustrated.

T. told me that at the outbreak of Civil War in 17th century Britain, legal control over the London printing press collapsed and there was suddenly an explosion of unofficial journals, broadsheets, and pamphlets. A London bookseller called George Thomason had the foresight to recognise that something extraordinary was happening and sent his employees out every day to collect every printed item they could find. The archive became the nucleus of the British library and one of the main collections of research materials for the period. Someone with similar foresight is needed here.

Budapest & Ljubljana

Wednesday December 20th
Evening

"Things are very tense here because of Romania," Istvan said. We were sitting in his beautiful tiled kitchen, coloured rugs, flowers painted on an old wooden cupboard, dried herbs above the sink, while he explained to us what was going on in Timisoara. A Hungarian protestant priest, an activist for Hungarian minority rights, had been asked to leave. Hundreds had gathered around his house in protest. When the police came, more gathered, then the army intervened. There were rumours of people being machine-gunned from helicopters and of revolts in other towns in Transylvania. No-one knew how many were dead.

"In Hungary, everyone is trying to outdo one another in the proving that they are the most patriotic. And the Communists, trying to compensate for their historical role are the most hysterical. The Free Democrats have in the past been accused of not being 'good Hungarians'. They have organised a march to Timisoara. It will take 3 days, Ceausescu came back from Tehran and accused Hungary of stirring up the Romanians. "Couldn't the march be made out to be a provocation?" I asked.

"The idea is that by the time they reach the border the regime will have fallen."

"That fast! Isn't it likely to get a lot bloodier first?" "Civil war almost certainly," Istvan replied with equanimity. "You don't seem at all bothered," I said, "aren't you worried about war?"

"Well, Romania has invaded us twice in this century, why not?, but Europe will protect us, particularly West Germany which is so grateful to us for opening our borders and letting all the East Germans out. So it will be a Hungarian German coalition just like in the war only this time *against* Romania." Istvan Rev is a professor of Economic History, small and dark and wiry with a dry sense of humour. It is quite impossible to tell if he is joking or not.

"Ceausescu will have to escape to China, otherwise they'll run motor cars over him and won't stop. The Warsaw Pact and Nato will form an alliance to invade another Warsaw Pact country . . . incredible – the end of the division of Europe!" He grinned and offered us some Tokaj.

"And what about Yugoslavia?" I asked T. "Oh, it will probably mobilise, the army is just waiting for the chance and I'll be called up," he said gloomily. Istvan wanted to hear about Czechoslovakia. "The last thing the party did here was to destroy itself so that people could not enjoy overthrowing it," he said, after listening to our descriptions of Prague. "There's not been any anti-Communist demonstrations here – only funerals. We have had three this year. We are living in the past, not in the future."

"At least you have a government?"

"I suppose we have a government. The Prime Minister has just resigned from the praesidium of the *new* Hungarian Socialist Party, which is losing members all the time. It had 170,000 before the congress in October. It has 50,000 now. And the *old* Hungarian Workers Party reformed on Sunday, having declared that its dissolution and the change of name was illegal. They have 80,000 members. In parliament deputies are leaving every day, either resigning or joining other parties. So we have Free Democrats in Parliament now." Istvan is a Free Democrat, the party to which most of the old intellectual opposition belong. "And we won the referendum to our surprise, why we don't know, but Democratic Forum is in disarray as they called for a boycott. So now the presidential election will be after the parliamentary elections. We don't want a presidential system, we want a parliamentary democracy." Istvan isn't standing as a deputy, he wants to keep a bit of distance.

Thursday December 21st
Budapest

Budapest feels strange after Prague. We wandered into the city centre to find disco music blaring and dancers modelling rather unpleasant clothes on an open air platform. There seem to be new boutiques everywhere and videos screens advertising yet more goods.

But the city is in mourning. There's a hunger strike outside the Romanian embassy, black flags hang from most public buildings and lighted candles are placed in windows. The church bells rang at 1.00 p.m. A woman in a pottery shop told me this afternoon that 'the scandal' was all over for the time being, but Istvan just called up the stairs after listening to the radio – "There are crowds in the street and corpses. Ceausescu tried to make a speech and had to retreat. Students are calling for a general strike and going to the factories to ask for support and people have taken over Timisoara and the army had to retreat."

Friday December 22nd
Budapest

The demonstration caught me by surprise. I had just made an appointment to get my hair cut when I heard shouting and clapping and turned to see a crowd coming down the street, waving Hungarian flags, arms outstretched in 'V' signs. "Ceausescu has gone!" said a blonde haired young woman in perfect English, smiling at my bewilderment. It turned out she was a tourist guide and happy to explain as we walked along. The demonstration had started as a mass this morning and had spontaneously turned into a celebration march when they heard the news. "We don't know where he's gone, he's trying to escape!" At the front men sat on a car waving Romanian flags. "Why are they torn?" I asked, "They've cut out the Communist symbol." A car with loudspeakers was playing an old Transylvanian hymn. Did I know Transylvania used to be part of Hungary? We walked past shops and offices, people leant over balconies and out of windows, clapping, making 'V' signs. Five women in white overalls crowded into a doorway, two visibly crying. "They are playing speeches from last year's demonstration about Romania" my guide said, "We are going to St Stephen's church. He was an eleventh century king. Last year we took the Hungarian flag there to pray that things would be better for Hungarians in Romania, now we are going to thank him."

We had paused in a square beside the river. Cirrhus cloud above the Buda hills lit up by an afternoon sun, the Danube very flat. A long speech was coming through the loud speakers and my guide gave me snippets, punctuating her remarks with boos and cheers as she felt appropriate, as did the rest of the crowd.

"Ceausescu and his wife have escaped. They wanted an aeroplane but couldn't find one. Now they are in a car and the government have asked people to try and capture them . . . the security forces have poisoned water in many of the villages (boos). The Hungarians have telegraphed all the embassies in surrounding countries to arrest Ceausescu if he arrives there (cheers) . . . Ceausescu has asked the North Koreans to come and help(boos)."

"Who is the new government?," "The old Minister of Finance I think, I don't know . . ."

"The priest is back in Timisoara (cheers) . . . you know it all started with a Hungarian priest?" My guide was smiling happily. "Isn't it incredible?" She looked up at the building behind us. "There is the Ministry of Information and here is Radio Free Europe, playing outside in the street!" We walked on towards the parliament. "The Romanians want to thank the Hungarians for their support." The demonstration had grown as darkness fell, as had the number of Hungarian flags. It now filled the street, stretching back out of sight: all kinds of people in smart fur coats, cheap anoraks, working clothes, felt hats. Most had lighted candles and were now singing hymns. The emotion was intense and slightly unnerving. "You know, only two days ago I thought it would be war with Romania," my guide said. "Hungarian Romanian friendship always!"

"Death to Ceausescu, Death to Ceausescu!" the crowd was chanting.

"Romania has invaded Hungary before hasn't it?" I said. "Yes, but we were friends in the war," she replied. It seemed churlish to point out that this friendship was based on a fascist alliance in the face of her obvious goodwill. The demonstration was at a standstill and I had to get my hair cut, but at the hairdresser everyone was crowded around a small portable TV transmitting Romanian television, pictures of a balcony, crowds . . . my hairdresser, tired face, dyed red hair, had her hands together in an attitude of prayer.

We were supposed to be taking Miklos and Tonshi out to dinner. Miklos Harasti, writer and former dissident, was standing for parliament as a Free Democrat. Tonshi had given up her job as a psychologist to be deputy campaign manager. When we got to their apartment, Miklos, distracted but friendly, rushed us in to watch Romanian television. The new government have apparently taken over the television station and the pictures flickered erratically from the studio, where a tense, nervous looking, oddly assorted crowd, some holding weapons and some torn flags, took it in turns to speak rapidly into a microphone, to a balcony from which various people called for calm and told an enormous crowd that "We are safe while you are here." There appeared to be shooting. A man appeared saying that he had got out of prison one hour ago. Back inside the studio a new group had appeared, one of whom read a long proclamation about the formation of a National Salavation Committee, the need for free elections, democracy and an end to terror. As he spoke, the crowd in the studio grew larger and someone conjured up the words, "TELEVIZUNEA ROMANA LIBERA". An army officer almost in tears took the microphone and another military man whose uniform seemed too big for him, with too much braid, was trying to push his way to the centre of the screen. Men who clearly knew where their best interests lay! There's something extraordinary about seeing another country's revolution on television, as it happens. It was like watching the strangest mixture of melodrama and comic opera. This is not TV drama however, it is real and the TV is an essential component, a key player in maintaining the reality, while the world watches. It's more addictive than any soap opera, even though I can't understand the language or identify the players.

"Incredible," Miklos kept saying. "It's just like '56." The camera had switched to men riding lorries, waving flags, books being thrown over balconies. "Don't burn the archives," Miklos muttered . . . "you know it all started with a Hungarian priest?" Tonshi arrived cheerful and exhausted looking. Miklos had to go, "his comrades were waiting," but first, the Hanuka candle had to be lit. We stood around the table, Nana his daughter lit the candle and Miklos in overcoat and scarf, cap on his head, read the blessing a little hurriedly then asked me to drive him to the office. In the car he talked about the elections. He didn't feel certain of getting in. "It's a multiparty system now, there are no guarantees. 75 parties, 7 important ones. Democratic Forum is definitely the strongest, perhaps 20,000, compared to our 10,000. We'll have to make a coalition with them after the election, otherwise this country will be ungovernable."

Outside the Free Democrats' office, there were a crowd of people with Hungarian and Romanian flags listening to the radio. Inside all the paraphenalia of a political campaign; glossy leaflets, telephones, copy machines, groups of people in earnest huddles, referendum posters pinned to the wall saying "Igen, Igen, Igen, Igen".

A friend told me this afternoon she wouldn't join any political party. An intelligent serious woman, she was tired of "all the manipulation." "Nobody authorised the Free Democrats to speak at the Round Table on our behalf. They just assumed they could. They wanted it both ways, to negotiate for us and when the Round Table agreement didn't go their way, to insist on a referendum. 'Let the people decide' they said, they are not honest." She had voted in the referendum. She didn't agree with the Communists, "but they want to make anyone who opposed Communism in the past a hero. My uncle was a soldier in '56. His Commander suddenly ordered them to a particular place and it turned out they were fighting Communists, of course he was imprisoned for it but he was obeying orders, not being a hero."

"Hungary should abolish its army," she added, "we don't need it. We could use U.N. forces if necessary. That's an issue for the new parties." She saw no chance of them taking it up.

Tonshi, who we finally got to take out to dinner, has no love for the political game either, but saw it as necessary. She was trying to co-ordinate relief trucks to Romania and wished people would co-ordinate their efforts rather than try to make political capital. "And look at Fidesz (the young democrats), refusing the money to which new political parties are entitled. They overestimate their strength and don't campaign. They think they'll simply be elected. Politics *cost money*." After the elections she is going back to her job.

Simecka quoted Churchill at us on Wednesday, I don't know how accurately, talking about the need for normal, multi-party democracy in Europe. "If no better form is available then we must use this bad form of political democracy." "There is no other way, I think." Simecka concluded.

He also identified however, young people's antagonism to "typical political ways" and wondered if they would build some other political forms for themselves.

Listening to him, Barbel, Janek Litynski and Vaclev Havel, and watching this extraordinary phenomenon of 'round tables', citizens commissions and forums, I too wonder if what might come out of this wave of transformation is, not a new ideology – there is a conscious rejection of ideology – but a quite new kind of political organisation, something that is neither parliamentary nor extra parliamentary. It is not just a question of language. Though I do believe ones language can strongly influence form, not just the other way around. Onyszkiewicz says people want to avoid the 'contamination' of the word 'party'; this doesn't mean they don't want political influence, it does mean they are looking for structural alternatives to something widely regarded as corrupt.

The Round Tables and sudden emergence of Citizens' Committees and Forums have given people the experience of being politically effective at State level, without the need to attach an ideological label; and an awareness that local problems can be solved in the same way. So it is not surprising that, as Janek described, in Poland they strongly resent what they perceive as "ideological" interference; and struggle to hang onto their autonomy, even from their own national leadership. The movements outside these structures are also looking for space. The Green Federation in Poland wrote an open letter to the parliament saying that political activity was as "natural as breathing" and should not be restricted in any way. Any new law on political parties had to provide an open space for new forms of political organisations, such as those without formal membership or internal power structures.

Janek talked of "enriching" parliamentary democracy through greater sensitivity to social movements. Simecka envisages normal political pluralism with greater influence from the informal movements. Jacek Szymanderkski sees these movements as breaking politics out of the old ideological straitjackets. The question is whether these local "committees" and movements feel forced to consolidate and transform themselves into parties in order to survive and compete with existing political forces; or whether, while maintaining informality and allowing fragmentation, they can still, firstly, allow for the development of what Barbel calls political consciousness, and, secondly, continue to be the basis for effective pressure on Government.

There is a growing awareness that certain crucial issues cannot be dealt with by ideological debate: whether it's militarism, aid to Romania, relations with the third world or ecological damage. Moreover, there is often a consensus on these issues that can't surface properly when people feel bound by party loyalty. Barbel said, "The problems of this century are not going to be solved by parties any more, only by people who group themselves around a problem and dedicate themselves to resolving it." Perhaps we really are at a point in Europe where we can move away from all the old 'isms', the debates about left and right – and focus on concrete issues: Hunger, violence, poverty, justice, freedom. Perhaps this is too much to hope for.

Sunday December 24th
Ljubljana

The city is wrapped in fog. The lovely soft coloured buildings in the old town are ghosts of themselves, looming over shoppers in the Christmas Market.

I am trying to accustom myself to shopping in millions of Dinars. Inflation is high, worse than Poland and people joke about paying for a meal at the beginning, as it will cost more by the end.

"Nothing much is going on," T.'s friend Marko says. Nothing much means that relations with Serbia are still frozen and martial law continues in Kosovo, although no one is actually being killed at this moment.

T. couldn't understand initially why Serbia is so supportive of the Romanian uprising, given their welcome to Ceausescu on a number of occasions and the stated anti Communist ideals of the National Salvation front. However it appears that the Serbs identify the uprising with their own demonstrations two years ago. They purged the party and installed Milosevic. He is not exactly the embodiment of pluralist democratic thinking; but I am always amazed at our ability to reframe historical and contemporary events to our own needs: Albanians demanding Human Rights are counter revolutionists, Romanians are Revolutionary heroes.

There are changes. A new democratic alliance has formed here in Slovenia and something similar in Serbia. T. is still gloomy. We will be "interesting" and newsworthy again. People will come and visit us, like a museum."

Monday December 25th
Ljubljana

It is very quiet here. The village sits on a smooth plateau of green felds. These are old mountains, no sharp edges. The landscape curves away in gentle lines, covered in beech forest. This morning we went to buy apples from the farm across the road. A large honey coloured building with wooden tiled barn, surrounded by orchard. The woman invited us in, insisting we waited in the rather cold and dark, best room, overlooked by photographs of severe looking relatives and a magnificent chandelier. "There are only two like it in Slovenia," she told us with pride, switching on the light so we could adire the handblown pink and yellow lilies and green leaves. This was a glass blowing area and they made it here. She offered us two kinds of plum Schnapps and settled down to drink some herself and tell us stories. How all the farms had had their own piece of forest and timber yards once, their main source of income. How the State, determined to deprive them of this economic independence had collectivised the industry – claiming ownership of the forest and insisting the men worked outside the village in a larger mill. How now the large mills couldn't work economically and were making men redundant and there was no way to establish the old patterns of existence . . . a sad story, cheerfully told. A small plump woman with dark eyes, her husband died last year, so she managed alone. It meant she had to sell the cow. She was worried we would mind such small 'marked' apples. They had no money for pesticides. We told her we were delighted.

At midnight mass last night the church was packed, people filling the aisles and overflowing into the courtyard. The priest, a youngish man in glasses told us to be joyful because today, Christmas Day, was a holiday for the first time snce the War, and to remember those suffering under, and fighting against tyranny, particularly in Romania.

I listen obsessively to the radio, where American intervention in

Panama competes with "continued shootings" in Romania. The Ceausescus have been caught. Someone told me that when Niku was caught he was put on television and the interviewer accused him of taking children hostages. "Only one child" he replied.

People will argue that Romania demonstrates that the non-violent overthrow of an absolute dictatorship is not possible. They will miss the essential point, that in Romania, as in the GDR, Czechoslovakia and Poland, non-violence was the key component. The timescale was different in each country but the dynamics the same. People demonstrated, they were violently repressed, they continued to demonstrate, frightened but determined, the demonstrations escalated and in the face of continued resistance, the regimes crumbled away. That's not to say that this crumbling away may not be accompanied by horrifying violence, but this would appear to be the last spiteful outburst of people whose days are numbered, and wish to wreak havoc and revenge before they go.

Of course the international context is crucial. Jan Urban was sure that one factor in the decision not to use the army in Czechoslovakia was the Soviets. He told us that the Soviets had an unnamed member of the Politbureau in Czechoslovakia, who at a crucial moment had insisted that "Czech sergeants were not going to spoil our USSR – USA disarmament talks" but international considerations are crucial in any revolution, violent or non-violent. As is the relationship between army and people, identified by Simecka, and the knowledge of other people's successful struggles. Simecka described the impact of "all those masses going away from East Germany, in Prague alone people could see thousand upon thousand. Every week you could see the regime dissolving itself. There was something in the air and young people's courage was growing and growing."

In the end, it would appear that a regime that has no other legitimation but the violence at its disposal cannot maintain itself, except by the continued use of that violence, and even that is finite, given that at some point the armed forces may no longer wish to be identified with illegitimate authority. The army seems to have switched sides after the first events in Timisoara but it was not the army who challenged Ceausescu, but unarmed civilians, booing him last Thursday. Collapse seems to come at the point where a large enough number of people, even in an atomised, fearful and impoverished society, are no longer prepared to co-operate with their own subjugation. Surely now it must begin to be clear that it is not tanks or nuclear weapons of any design that liberate. It is people's personal courage and their preparedness not to threaten others but to risk their *own* lives, that increases the sum of freedom and human dignity in the world.

Tuesday December 26th

I turned on the World Service this morning to hear that Ceausescu and his wife have been executed after a secret trial. And that "this brings to an end a phase in the post War history of Europe."

Outside there are tits in the orchard and the mechanical tapping of a woodpecker. It is mild and sunny and yet I cannot shake off a feeling of horror. The hatred is understandable, I thought they might be shot when captured but why this secret trial, and calculated death. And now "videos of the execution" will be shown . . .

In Wroclaw, weeks ago (though it seems like years) in that argument Adam Michnik had on the stairs, with the Russian who wanted to hang everyone, there was another Russian who said "the task of our victory will be, not to be the same as those before." And Adam said, "I am afraid of people who wish to judge, I am afraid of this."